BLOODLINES

GREAT WINEMAKING FAMILIES OF THE WORLD

& GRAPEVINES

BLOODLINES

GREAT WINEMAKING FAMILIES OF THE WORLD

& GRAPEVINES

Jonathan Ray

Photographs by **Jason Lowe**

IN ASSOCIATION WITH

BERRY BROS & RUDD

For Marina, with love

First published in 2004 by Conran Octopus Limited
a part of Octopus Publishing Group
2–4 Heron Quays, London E14 4JP
www.conran-octopus.co.uk

Publishing Director: Lorraine Dickey
Art Director: Chi Lam
Executive Editor: Zia Mattocks
Art Editor: Sam Chick
Editor: Helen Ridge
Production Manager: Angela Couchman

British Library Cataloguing-in-Publication Data.
A catalogue record for this book is available from the British Library.

ISBN 1 84091 301 0

Printed in China

Contents

Introduction

There's an affinity, somehow, between wine and family businesses. My family has been selling the stuff for over 300 years, since the time it was sold by the cask, and the glass bottles were always worth more than the vinous contents. Most of it has been made by the kind of families that Jonathan Ray and Jason Lowe illustrate in this book. Family businesses are nowadays looked upon as oddities. It comes as a shock to learn that 80 per cent of all companies in the world are family firms; that, far from being the exception, they are the rule. The high profile of the multinationals and the conglomerates seems to overshadow them. But even this is a distortion. It is true that the vast majority of companies are corner shops and one-man bands, first- or second-generation affairs that struggle to exist. But the success of a few sways the statistics back again: think of Johnson & Johnson, BMW, Walmart and Tetrapack. Over half of the world's wealth is earned by family firms. We are the norm. We are the reality. The rest are pale imitations. From a perspective within a family business, it doesn't always feel that way.

All families are unique, and my family is more unique than yours, or yours, or yours – and a brief glance at the many varied personalities that leap from the following pages will prove that point. The differences between them – and the ways in which they run their businesses – are staggering. For example, they come from all corners of the globe. It would be impossible to confine this book to the 'Old World' – that is, France, Spain, Portugal and Germany, with a nod towards Italy – as would have been the case in my grandfather's day. Yet many of the further-flung vineyards were started by families that were British in origin, but certainly not all – the Dalmatian wine dynasties of New Zealand are central to that country's rapid rise to success, for example. Curiously enough, only one of the 'New World' companies featured has its roots in European winemaking – and that family clearly has a tendency to think of itself as English by inclination. To balance it out, one of the French families is still firmly Irish at heart.

Right centre: Berry Bros. & Rudd has traded from its current address – 3 St James's Street in London – since it was established in 1698. The company has supplied the British Royal family since the reign of George III, and is currently the holder of Royal Warrants to both the Queen and the Prince of Wales. Since 1923, when BB&R created Cutty Sark Scots Whisky, there has always been an international dimension to the business. This has been underlined in recent years by the company's wine shops in Heathrow airport, Dublin and Hong Kong, an operation in Japan, and its award-winning website, www.bbr.com, which caters to customers throughout the world. Traditional and at the same time forward-thinking, Berry Bros. & Rudd is proud of its reputation as one of the most successful and enduring family companies operating today.
Right: Many members of the two owning families, Berry and Rudd, are working in, or intimately involved with, the firm. Clockwise, from top left: Simon Berry, deputy chairman; Jane Berry Green, wife of Christopher Berry Green; Edward Rudd, John Rudd's son; Christopher Berry Green, chairman; Geordie d'Anyers Willis, Simon Berry's nephew; David Berry Green, Christopher Berry Green's son.
Left: John Rudd, the IPC (immediate past chairman), still sits on the board of the company that he led from 1985 to 2001.

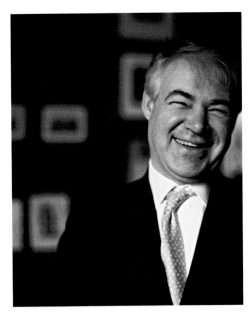

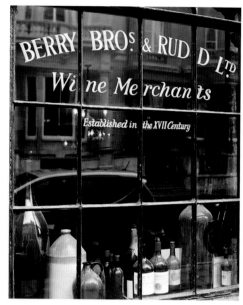

There is no set pattern to the histories of these families, either. Some are long-established dynasties, some are establishing themselves in their first or second generation. Some are still farmers, proud of their hands-on connection with the soil and the roots that sustain them; some are aristocrats, overseeing their estates from a lofty distance.

Some eke out a meagre existence from their vineyards; some have grown extremely rich from their own efforts and their family's before them. Others have made fortunes in different industries, and are now using those fortunes to fund their passion for making wine. For every proprietor whose grandfather made wine there is another who started life as a lawyer, an accountant or a nuclear scientist.

Some are tightly knit families, where the grandchildren pick grapes from vineyards named after their grandparents. Some have less cordial relations with their relations, and seem to abide by Oscar Wilde's dictum: 'God gives us our families. Thank God we can choose our friends for ourselves.'

So, with all these differences, what is it that unites these stories?

It all boils down, I believe, to a sense of continuity. The bottle of wine that I sell today is the product of the weather pattern of 12 long months, of a vine that might have been growing for 50 years, of a vineyard that might have been planted 200 years previously, of a region that might have been recognized as suitable for the cultivation of grapes 2,000 years ago. Even if the vineyard is comparatively new, the geological and climatic factors that make it special were certainly ordained millennia ago.

Furthermore, it is possible that this bottle will not be drunk today, or next year, or even in my lifetime. In our cellars in St James's Street we have bottles that were sealed when my great-great-great-grandfather's name was above the shop. In order to truly understand the nature of wine, one has to have a sense of the passing of time.

Within the context of a publicly owned company, this makes little sense. Shareholders demand results today, not next year, and employees have their eyes firmly set on hitting their annual targets and collecting this year's bonus. To a family-owned private company, however, the affinity is inescapable. We are creating something today with the gifts we have inherited from our predecessors, which should benefit the generations yet to come. In life, as in business.

At Harvard Business School, that temple to the corporate ideal, they are now teaching students that there is much to be learnt from the model of the family business. In an era when the crash of the dot coms and the corruption that destroyed Enron is still a recent memory, an examination of the values inherent in family companies is very timely. After all, every business was a family business once.

It hasn't been easy choosing which estates to feature in this book. We could have simply focussed on the world's most famous family wineries, but these have had their stories told many times. Instead, Jonathan Ray and I decided that we would pick one family from each of the world's great winegrowing regions, and that for every well-known winery we would feature a less well-known one; for every long-established property we would have a new one; and for every large one, a small one. Sadly, some old friends didn't make the cut.

Although there are some surprising differences between the final nineteen estates, there are also many even more surprising similarities. But, most importantly, what the families do have in common is that they all have fascinating stories to tell and they all make wines of the highest quality. I only wish that Berry Bros. & Rudd stocked them all!

Deputy Chairman, Berry Bros. & Rudd

Above: With its structure dating back to Tudor times, the premises of 3 St James's Street are part of the soul of Berry Bros. & Rudd. Little has apparently changed since this photograph was taken in 1925.

Opposite, clockwise from top left: As many as 70 people can dine in the vaulted cellars. The large Georgian shop windows are a London landmark. Photographs of previous generations line the stairs leading down to the cellars. Slate boards record the precious bottles for sale. Ancient bottles in the House Reserves lie behind lock and key: vintages of Tokay stretch back to 1834, of Cognac to 1811. Above the fireplace in the parlour at the back of the shop are even older bottles, albeit empty. These date, however, from a time when the cost of glass made the bottle always more precious than its contents.

Brown Brothers

King Valley, Australia

The village of Milawa sprawls across a dusty crossroads on the main Sydney to Melbourne road in the heart of the Australian bush, where Ned Kelly and his gang once ran riot. It is here, in 1885, that Scottish émigré John Francis Brown decided to settle and plant some Riesling, Muscat and Shiraz in the foothills of the Victorian Alps.

In those tentative early days John Francis counted himself lucky if he managed to sell a couple of bottles of sweet 'sherry' to a passer-by. Times have changed, though, and today Brown Brothers produces some 600,000 cases of wine per year and exports to more than 25 countries. The company has long been at the forefront of the Australian winegrowing revolution, which has taken us from the grim days of Kanga Rouge and Wallaby White to the remarkable situation where more Australian wine than French is now consumed in the UK.

When Mark Walpole, chief viticulturalist at Brown Brothers, takes visitors on a tour of the vineyards, he adopts a tongue-in-cheek approach, which helps put the massive scale of the Brown Brothers enterprise into a European context. 'Right,' he will say as he drives south out of Milawa. 'We're now driving from the Southern Rhône up to Burgundy. And now we're off to Bordeaux and, finally, high in the mountains, here we are in Alsace en route to Champagne.' It is not as bizarre as it sounds because, although it can be bakingly hot here in high summer, the Brown Brothers vineyards do indeed encompass all the climates and soil types associated with those European wine regions. This quirk of geography, along with a hearty dollop of the Australian 'can-do' attitude, enables the company to follow a philosophy that would startle many a winegrower in the Côte d'Or, Tuscany or the Mosel.

Brown Brothers is the antithesis of an Old World winery and, indeed, many New World ones, in that it produces over 100 different wines (red, white, still, sparkling, sweet, dry and fortified) each year from, astoundingly, 50 different grape varieties. Alongside the classic varieties such as Cabernet Sauvignon, Merlot, Pinot Noir, Shiraz, Chardonnay, Riesling, Sauvignon Blanc and Semillon, Brown Brothers also grows less obvious varieties such as Barbera, Dolcetto, Nebbiolo, Tempranillo, Moscato, Pinot Grigio and Orange Muscat, to name but a handful. And although the family vineyards stretch as far as the eye can see – covering some 610 hectares (1,500 acres) – over 60 per cent of the annual crop is bought in from a hundred or so outside growers. So great is the number of grape varieties used by the company that the harvest can take up to three months, with the winery in operation 24 hours a day during the peak six to eight weeks of the vintage.

The work is all extremely high tech: each vineyard boasts its own weather station linked to a central computer at Milawa, ensuring that the winemaking team keeps up to date with information about wind, humidity, rainfall and frost. Unfortunately, this is no guard against vineyard pests, which include wallabies munching the grapes, kangaroos attacking the canes and wombats digging holes in the rows between the vines, causing damage to tractors and picking machines.

At Brown Brothers, the winegrowers' sacred tenet that *terroir* is all is turned on its head, for it is the sales and marketing team that determines the planting strategy of the company with its 'grape requirement plan'. They identify which grape varieties are coming into vogue, and Mark Walpole and the chief winemaker, Terry Barnett, plant accordingly. Early trend-spotting is vital because it takes five years to propagate, plant, harvest and vinify the first crop of fruit.

'At the moment, Tempranillo and Viognier are extremely popular,' says Mark, 'so I'm searching for places to plant more of them, while we dig up the Gewurztraminer, which has fallen out of favour. I look at climate – which, crucially, must be frost-free – then soil type and then availability of water.' It is a philosophy of have land, will plant. 'It might not always be quite the right soil,' he continues, 'but at least the climate will be spot on. And it's amazing what you can do when you have unlimited access to water.'

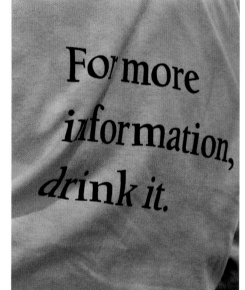

For more information, drink it.

Terry Barnett's predecessor as winemaker, John Graham Brown, also relished this go-getting approach: 'I'm afraid I can't help thinking that growing just one variety year in, year out – such as Riesling in Germany – must be a bit like milking a cow.' Ask any member of the Brown family why the company grows so many different grape varieties and produces so many different types of wine, and they will look at you rather pityingly and say, 'Because we can.'

Although it was John Francis who started everything back in the 19th century, it is his son, John Charles Brown, and John Charles's wife, Patricia, who are credited with making Brown Brothers the company it is today. 'My husband always seemed to have a crystal ball that predicted what people would be drinking ten years before they knew themselves,' says Patricia.

There was great sadness in May 2004 when John Charles Brown passed away, aged 89. He and Patricia, who were born within four days of each other in 1915, had made their home a mile or so from the winery and continued to take a keen interest in the business long after their retirement. Despite being very frail in his later years, John Charles retained a sharp sense of humour and, although modest about his own contribution to Brown Brothers, was intensely proud of the family firm. 'We never thought the business would grow this big,' he joked not long before he died. 'We just thought we'd plant a few grapes and see how we got on. It's these sons of ours who've made the company what it is, conning all these poor people into drinking our wine!'

John Charles joined his father on the farm in 1933 at a time when most of the production was devoted to fortified wines. He was subsequently joined by his four sons: John Graham, Peter, Ross and Roger (who has since died). John Charles retired as CEO in 1988 aged 73, and was succeeded by John Graham, who held the post for 13 years. John Graham, in turn, became chairman, making Ross the CEO. Peter is also on the board of directors, but sold some shares to his brothers to finance his purchase of All Saints vineyard in Wahgunyah, northern Victoria. Recently a fourth generation joined the firm: John Andrew Brown and Cynthia Brown, John Graham's two children, are the chief information officer and employment services manager respectively.

To join the firm, family members must be well educated, preferably to university level, and have spent four years working elsewhere, either inside or outside the wine world. 'We're not in the business of creating jobs for the next generation,' stresses Ross. 'If they want to work here, they've got to prove themselves. We can't make "soft seats" for anyone.'

In 1989 Brown Brothers instituted their Kindergarten Winery, a research and development facility to explore new varieties and wine styles. Here experiments are carried out on new blends and varieties before they are released via the Cellar Door – the on-site wine shop visited annually by 100,000 people, which is more than go to gawp at Uluru (Ayers Rock). Next to the Cellar Door is the Epicurean Centre, where visitors and those who have just bought some wine can lunch or dine. The food is matched to the wine, rather than the wine to the food, with the menu listing the wine first, followed by the dish recommended to accompany it. Brown Brothers also has an extensive database of recipes, which can be drawn upon when someone buys a wine and wants to know what to eat with it. Customers are encouraged to linger over their glasses of wine under the trees outside, and even to cook their own meals on specially constructed barbecues. This all fits in with the family atmosphere at Brown Brothers and the company's mission to educate its customers to the delights of food and wine.

Brown Brothers also has another, much more commercial, reason for encouraging visitors to the Cellar Door. 'We recognize that wine is a fashion industry and so we have to plan ahead, and the reaction from our Cellar Door customers is invaluable,' says Ross. 'They vote with their pockets and

Opposite: The family prepares to spread the word at an annual wine event in Perth, Western Australia, far from their base near Melbourne, but still among friends. The late John Charles Brown and his wife Patricia (middle right) enjoy the family activities. Patricia continues to take a close interest in the business, even as she approaches her nineties.

Below: Peter Brown is a keen pilot and keeps his plane at the airfield over the road from the Brown Brothers winery. There are plans to develop the strip to encourage more weekending visitors from Melbourne.

provide us with an accurate opinion poll. We're playing around with Tempranillo at the moment, and so far our Cellar Door customers seem to love it. When we get a reaction like this, we are usually prepared to take a commercial risk.' The Cellar Door wines have a certain cachet with their unique pencil-sketch labels, which are not available on the company's other wines. Customers who buy them can boast to their friends that they have the wines before they have reached the shops.

Some wines in the Cellar Door get tweaked and re-issued after feedback from the public, while others get the thumbs down and don't get marketed, no matter how much the winemakers try to push them. All sorts of curiosities have been fine-tuned at the Kindergarten Winery and Cellar Door: a Dolcetto and Syrah blend; a Chardonnay, Sauvignon Blanc and Pinot Grigio blend; a remarkable sparkling Shiraz; and, most successfully of all, Tarrango, the unique Australian variety bred by crossing the Portuguese red grape Touriga Naçional with the white grape Sultana. Tarrango was developed jointly by Brown Brothers and scientists from the Commonwealth Scientific and Industrial Research Organization in an effort to produce a light, fresh red wine ideal for summer drinking. This Australian answer to Beaujolais, best served lightly chilled, has been a runaway success and has since become one of Brown Brothers' best-selling wines. The company hopes that current experiments with Cienna, a cross between Cabernet Sauvignon and Sumoll, will be just as successful.

The latest innovation to come from the Kindergarten Winery is the range named after the inspirational Patricia Brown. Launched in March 2003, the Patricia Range is a selection of six wines: a sparkler, a Chardonnay, a Cabernet Sauvignon, a Merlot, a Shiraz and a Noble Riesling, all designed to bring the name of Brown Brothers to a wider audience. 'With the Patricia range we are in pursuit of excellence,' says Ross Brown. 'We want the wines to show vintage differences, with each wine bearing the winemaker's individual stamp and style. Perhaps Brown Brothers' wines have sometimes been perceived as fairly safe, without ever having made the earth move, in which case we hope this new range will show our true capabilities.'

Ross certainly thinks that they are in a strong position, especially in relation to European winemakers. 'Europe is regulating itself out of the market in my view. They pass down parcels of vineyards to their children that are too small to produce wine in quantity, and the laws are far too bureaucratic. The same varieties have been grown for centuries, with legislation ensuring that new varieties cannot be introduced. I came back from visiting the European wine regions in 1996 all fired up, thinking that Australia was *the* place to grow wine. The costs are huge in Europe, and I think that we do it better and cheaper over here. I was sent packing 20 years ago with the "colonial cringe" and was told that my wine didn't taste like Pouilly Fumé. I told them that it wasn't meant to. The Old World reacts to history and tradition; the New World reacts to its customers.'

With the three Brown brothers on the board and with their children being groomed to take their places, the family succession is assured. The company's everyday wines are selling well, novel wines such as Tarrango are being rapturously received, and the Patricia Range should bring the family name to a new type of customer. And should tastes change, the company's flexibility in the market place, coupled with its skills in the vineyard and winery, mean that it is better equipped than many to adapt.

Not only that, everyone in the family loves what they are doing. They live the good life and make a product to be proud of. As John Andrew says, 'Brown Brothers has very high ideals and everything we do, we do bloody well. We're not making crushed gravel or widgets here; what we do is fun, and so it should be! I don't believe that there is a more diverse wine region in the world. We could make more money by not concentrating on the weird varieties and hybrids, or we could just make Chardonnay and nothing else, but where's the joy in that? Living here is an absolute delight. I have a beautiful house on a mountain side with views on three sides of over 100km (62 miles). It's a wonderful climate and I only work a 15-minute drive from home. I have a lovely wife and two lovely kids. I get to travel a bit and I suppose the only stress that I feel is worrying about hitting a wombat on the road as I drive home at the end of the day.'

Above: Even the youngest members of the family are dragooned into helping out at the big al fresco tastings. Here, seven-year-old John Yeo Brown, son of John Andrew Brown, grabs some well-earned refreshment.

Right: The Australian flag flutters above the corrugated iron roof of the Old Barn, where it all started in 1885. The company's new Patricia range of wines (bottom right) is named after Patricia Brown, the family matriarch who arrived in Milawa in 1939 with her new husband John Charles Brown. 'The changes since we started have been incredible,' she says. 'We just thought that we had four boys and we had to have something to hand on to them, but we had no idea that we were starting a so-called dynasty. It is just incredible what the boys have achieved, and I was astonished and delighted when I was told that the new range of wines was to be named after me. Astonished and delighted.'

PATRICIA

LATE HARVESTED
NOBLE RIESLING
1999

Leeuwin Estate

Margaret River, Australia

I t would be fair to say that Denis Horgan, the jovial founder of Leeuwin Estate in Margaret River, Western

Australia, never misses a trick. Now in his middle sixties, Denis positively pops and fizzes with ideas, schemes and

plans, and for someone who left school at 14 with no further education other than accountancy training and a spell

at what he refers to as the University of HK&T (Hard Knocks & Travel), Denis hasn't done badly.

**Above: Denis Horgan in characteristic pose –
in mid-anecdote, glass in hand. 'None of us in
Margaret River went into wine to make money,'
he says. 'We all had other jobs. We all just
wanted to make the best wine in the world.'
Opposite: The Margaret River district features
pristine white sandy beaches, a spectacular
coastline and amazing waves. Although Denis
doesn't surf as much as he used to, he still
heads off to the ocean most days with
whomever he can round up for a quick dip.
Previous page: Leeuwin Estate lies 300km
(180 miles) south of Perth, surrounded by
majestic forests of eucalyptus and karri trees.**

He qualified as an accountant and built up a highly profitable practice, had extensive mining and energy interests (with which he made a lot of money, lost it and made it again) and, thanks to a chance encounter with the great Robert Mondavi 30 years ago, is the proprietor of one of Australia's finest and most lauded wineries. Oh, and he is also a successful impresario, having founded a dazzlingly successful series of internationally acclaimed concerts – of which more later – and he has plans to build a golf course and a five-star hotel. When told that he seems to have a finger in lots of different pies, Denis, who is not what you would call a shrinking violet, roars with laughter, saying, 'Yeah, well, I suppose you could say that I'm a bit of a lateral thinker!'

Denis was born and brought up in Perth and, as a young surfer, regularly drove the three hours south to Margaret River, chasing the region's celebrated great waves. On one such trip he came across a beautiful estate for sale. 'My wife Tricia and I both fell instantly in love with the place and just knew that we had to buy it,' he says. At that time – 1969 – the area was known as the 'medical belt', owing to the number of doctors who lived there. The thought of making wine had never entered anyone's head. The couple bought the property, renaming it Leeuwin Estate, and spent a great deal of their time there, with their four children: Rebecca, Justin, Simone and Christian. The estate is in an idyllic location, surrounded by spice-scented forests of red gum and karri trees. Kookaburras cackle away in the branches while kangaroos lope by, and the converging Indian and Southern Oceans break their spectacular waves on long sandy beaches.

'And so there I was,' recalls Denis, 'minding my – or rather minding someone else's – business, when a friend called to say that some American bloke called Robert Mondavi was interested in buying our property. I hadn't a clue who he was, so I sent my secretary to the library to see what she could find out about him. We had no intention of selling the place – we regarded it as our home – but after discovering who this chap was, we thought that if Bob Mondavi was interested in growing wine in Margaret River, then growing wine in Margaret River must be something worth doing.' So, instead of selling the property, Denis and Tricia decided to create a vineyard for themselves, despite not knowing the first thing about wine. Mondavi, although thwarted in his attempts to buy the estate, magnanimously agreed to act as the Horgans' guide and mentor.

The first vines were planted in 1973, and from the outset the plan was to make wines that would rank with the best in the world. Mondavi insisted that the Horgans find a young winemaker whom they could send to California and Europe for training. This experience would enable the winemaker to dictate the style of wine that the estate should produce. Bob Cartwright was that lucky man, and he has been the winemaker at Leeuwin ever since. Thanks to Bob's education in several different wine regions, Leeuwin's wines have always been made in an international rather than an Australian style, which, Denis believes, has helped them steal a march on some of their fellow countrymen's wines.

'We were pioneers and had no idea which variety would come out on top,' says Denis. 'It was all a bit of a lottery.' Initially Gewürztraminer, Chardonnay, Riesling, Cabernet Sauvignon, Pinot Noir and Shiraz were planted over some 89 hectares (220 acres). They soon found that they had planted Shiraz

Left: The restaurant at Leeuwin has received almost as many awards as the estate's wines, and tables on the balcony are much sought-after by diners. Above: Denis and Tricia Horgan have four children and six grandchildren, making family occasions often noisy affairs.

in the wrong spot and put Sauvignon Blanc there instead. The Gewurztraminer did well, but it was next door to the best position for growing Chardonnay. Pursuing the Horgans' stated aim to make the best possible wine in the world, they grafted the Gewurztraminer to Chardonnay, for which they would also get a better price (Denis is an accountant, remember) and bought another property further south for planting more Shiraz for a Rhône-style wine.

The estate's first commercial vintage was in 1979. 'I knew from day one that our wine was brilliant,' says Denis, 'because everyone was raving about it.' The so-called Art Series – the wine labels are identified with paintings commissioned from leading contemporary Australian artists, in much the same manner as the Ch Mouton Rothschild labels – represents the winery's finest wines from each vintage, and the Chardonnays and Cabernet Sauvignons have gained outstanding international acclaim. Indeed, the winery was immediately thrust into the forefront of the wine world when *Decanter* magazine gave its highest recommendation to the 1981 Art Series Chardonnay in a blind tasting. The Art Series wines are designed to age well, while the estate's Prelude Vineyards wines are intended for early drinking. The Siblings range of wines was launched recently, so-named to celebrate the involvement of the Horgans' children in the family business. In all, Leeuwin Estate produces about 70,000 cases a year, and exports to more than 30 countries – not bad for a winery and a wine region that have been producing wine for barely 30 years.

Denis is quick to admit that they weren't the first to make wine in Margaret River, but along with Cullen, Cape Mentelle, Moss Wood and Vasse Felix, Leeuwin Estate is regarded as one of the founding wineries of the region. Margaret River is not a region for making bulk wine; its production accounts for only two per cent of Australia's total production, but for 23 per cent of Australia's premium wine. 'We produce 0.06 per cent of Australia's wines at Leeuwin, which I guess is about the same amount that Brown Bros spills each year,' Denis laughs. 'We couldn't even begin to compete with such wineries in terms of size, so we've always made it our business to pursue excellence, and our marketing and publicity has to reflect that.'

And so it was that Denis Horgan came up with one of his many thumpingly good brainwaves: the Leeuwin Estate Concert Series. The London Philharmonic Orchestra was the first to perform. This occurred quite by chance when the Australian leg of the orchestra's world tour was thrown into

jeopardy and the Horgans, never slow to spot a good marketing opportunity, offered to underwrite the cost of the tour in return for the orchestra playing a date at Leeuwin. Denis had always been aware of the potential for staging concerts in the estate's natural outdoor amphitheatre, with its serried vines and gangling gum trees, and the barracking kookaburras, which are notorious for trying to compete vocally with the performers. 'Everyone thought that I was this big dreamer with little grasp on reality and that the concerts would never take off. The trouble is that, in retrospect, I don't think I was a big enough dreamer. If I had known how popular they would become, I'd have put the concert bowl further up the hill where there is more room. Nevertheless, this site is pretty amazing.'

Since that first concert in 1985, stars as diverse as Ray Charles, Diana Ross, Tom Jones, Dame Kiri Te Kanawa, Julio Iglesias, Dame Shirley Bassey and Bryn Terfel, as well as the Berlin Staatskapelle and the Czech Philharmonic, have performed at Leeuwin. 'The concerts are paid for out of our publicity budget. The philosophy is quite simple: we want those who attend to have a wonderful time, and we want 13,000 apostles leaving here once the concerts are over,' says Denis. 'Other wineries have tried to copy us but usually they make the mistake of trying to make money out of their concerts and other non-wine related activities. We don't. It's about frills, but wine remains absolutely the focus. I don't like to blow our own trumpet but if it wasn't for our marketing skills, a winery our size would have been dead long ago. An accountancy background isn't a bad place to start being a winegrower!'

Denis's fertile brain is constantly coming up with ideas. He talks of building a de luxe hotel on the estate, complete with an 18-hole championship golf course (Denis is rather keen on his golf, and plays each year in what he calls his local club's MASH Classic – the Mature-Aged Slicers and Hookers), which will be served by the existing airfield that Denis plans to develop further.

The roles of the Horgans' four children in all of these schemes are vital, although none of the family is directly involved as a winemaker. Simone is in charge of marketing, Justin is the financial controller and Rebecca oversees the concerts. Christian works as a broadcaster in Perth, but even he is press-ganged to help out with some aspect of the business when he comes to visit.

'A family business should complement the family, not destroy it,' Denis explains. 'We deliberately don't have any of my children as winemaker or viticulturalist – they're not scientifically inclined in any event. But we didn't want to be in the position of having to sack one of our kids if they turned out to be no good. I like to think that we're always ahead of our time here at Leeuwin, but we're not impatient. We develop our ideas, put them away and wait until the time is right to slot them in. When we're dead, all our children will have to do is open the safe and it will all be in there for them to put into action. And if they want to sell the business, we've even put down on paper the best way of doing that, too. Basically, I think that we've put in place ways of preventing the classic rags to riches to rags in three generations. We think big but we never lose sight of the fact that Leeuwin Estate is a wine business, and everything we do and have ever done is to complement the wine and to bring it to a wider audience.'

Denis and Tricia are more entrepreneurs than they are a winemakers or accountants, and had they not met Robert Mondavi, they might never have become involved in wine at all. But thanks to their remarkable ingenuity and tenacity, they have ended up in charge of one of the world's finest wineries and an ever-expanding business empire. Denis is utterly content with his lot, confident that he and Tricia have given their four children and six grandchildren a great start. As he sits on the restaurant balcony, wreathed in smiles as ever and a glass of wine in his hand, he considers his legacy.

'In my view, you don't have to know how anything in particular works; you just have to know the people who *do* know how such things work – and meeting Bob Mondavi changed our lives. I'm proud of what we have achieved here in such a short time, and I know that we produce a world-class wine. We have a wonderful life here, and as for our children, well, at least we're not condemning them to peer down people's throats and fix their dentures.'

Opposite: **Denis Horgan hopes that the next generation of the family will take on the challenge of running Leeuwin Estate. 'We can't rule from the grave,' he says, 'even though we have left carefully drawn-up plans for future schemes.' Ten years ago, the estate was doubled in size in order that it would be big enough to provide income and jobs for the growing family.**
Below: **Denis and Tricia Horgan have worked as a team at Leeuwin Estate from the very beginning, with Tricia becoming the full-time managing director as soon as the children were raised. The couple's joint development of the estate – and their contribution in general to the wine and tourism industries – was recognized in 2001 when they were both appointed Members of the Order of Australia.**

Viña Errázuriz

Aconcagua Valley, Chile

Chile has recently made the awkward leap from producing sound but unremarkable wines to making wines of real excellence. One of the people at the forefront of the country's winemaking revolution is 44-year-old Eduardo Chadwick, the president of Viña Errázuriz, who is currently living in England raising his company's profile, promoting his wines and studying for his Master of Wine exam.

Below: Eduardo Chadwick, president of Chilean wine producers Viña Errázuriz. Opposite: The Don Maximiano Estate is in a spectacular situation in the Aconcagua Valley at the foot of the Andes. The vineyards are planted with such varieties as Cabernet Franc, Cabernet Sauvignon, Merlot and Syrah, all of which thrive in the well-drained, shallow, rocky soils and sub-humid Mediterranean climate. Previous page: The vineyard at Viñedo Chadwick was once Don Alfonso Chadwick-Errázuriz's private polo field.

Watching him take tea in the garden of his Oxford home, surrounded by his wife, María, and four daughters, one would never imagine that Eduardo Chadwick was anything other than the quintessential English gentleman. Debonair and well-read, he might even pass for a don at Oxford University. He is, however, Chilean, thanks to his great-great-grandfather, Thomas Chadwick, a mining engineer who emigrated from England to Chile in the 1840s. Disappointed in his search for Chilean gold, Thomas found instead a Chilean wife – Dolores – thus establishing the South American branch of the Chadwick family, of which Eduardo represents the fifth generation.

Eduardo's English pedigree is so fine that he can trace his ancestry back through a host of worthies all the way to the Domesday Book and a knight who was granted land by a grateful William the Conqueror, and he retains a great affection for the country of his ancestors.

'I love England,' he says. 'I really love it. Britain and Chile have close historical links and I feel very at home here. I have also found it useful to move here for a while and see the world wine market from a different vantage point. But I must admit that simply being able to send the girls to school here would have been enough reason for my wife and me to live in England. I just wish the climate between October and February could be better.'

That Eduardo is president of Viña Errázuriz is thanks to Thomas Chadwick's grandson, Don Alejandro Chadwick, who married Leonor Errázuriz in 1909. Their son, the late Don Alfonso Chadwick-Errázuriz, was Eduardo's father. The Errázuriz family is one of the most notable in Chile and one that has played significant roles in the most important cultural, social and political events of the country, providing four Presidents of the Republic, two Archbishops of Santiago and countless writers, politicians, industrialists and diplomats. It was Don Maximiano Errázuriz, the great uncle of Eduardo's grandmother, who founded Viña Errázuriz in 1870.

Having made a fortune with his mining interests, Don Maximiano fulfilled his ambition of planting vines, choosing a striking position in the Aconcagua Valley at the foot of the Andes, some 100km (62 miles) north of Santiago, where the cool, rainy winters, hot, dry summers and moist Pacific Ocean breezes were found to be ideal.

Don Maximiano's estate is no longer inhabited, but instead the beautifully restored building is used for tastings, entertaining and for staging visits to the brand new winery built alongside. Apart from a 20-year 'hiccup', when it was owned by a bank, the Don Maximiano Estate has always remained in the hands of the same family. In 1983 it was bought back from the bank by Eduardo's father, who invited his son, who was then 23 years old, to join him in the firm as managing director.

Left: When the Chadwicks are not in Oxford their home is a town house in Santiago. The two great family estates of Don Maximiano and Viñedo Chadwick are used for entertaining journalists, wine merchants and importers. Both of these estates are beautifully kept, and while the former is stunningly sited in the shadow of the Andes, the latter makes up for its situation in the Santiago suburbs by feeling more like a family home, with Don Alfonso's hunting trophies on the walls, sporting mementos on the tables and the stables outside still bearing the names of his polo ponies.

Right: The Chadwicks en famille in Oxford. In the centre, Eduardo and his wife, María Eugenia, with (from left to right) their eldest daughter, also called María Eugenia, who holds a photograph of her late brother Juan Eduardo, Alejandra, María Jose and Magdalene.

Eduardo had studied industrial engineering in Santiago, but he knew a bit about wine through helping to tend the vines on his father's farm and from his travels through the Napa Valley and around Europe's wine-growing regions, which included a spell studying oenology in Bordeaux. Eduardo stresses that he is not a winemaker, but the knowledge he gained was crucial for his role in the company.

During the bank's tenure the winery closed, although the vineyards still existed. The equipment was elderly and unsophisticated, a problem that was prevalent throughout the Chilean wine industry, owing to old-fashioned techniques and lack of investment. On retrieving the property, the Chadwicks set about transforming the winery into one that was capable of producing top quality wines. On Don Alfonso's death in 1993, Eduardo became president of Viña Errázuriz, determined to continue what his father had started. He remained adamant that Chile had the potential to compete with the best.

'The challenge was to move away from everyday wine and to concentrate instead on making fine wine,' he says. 'And all the elements were there – climate, *terroir*, tradition – they all just needed to be exploited. So we concentrated on expanding the vineyards, on clone selection and on studying *terroir* in greater depth, and I have to say that it has paid off handsomely.'

Eduardo is especially committed to this concept of *terroir* – 'From the best land, the best wine,' as Don Maximiano used to say – and the idea that each vineyard imparts its own distinct characteristics to the grapes grown there. In knowledge of this, he extended the vineyards of Viña Errázuriz in the Aconcagua Valley and modernized its technology and machinery, as well as developing other estates in the valley and beyond, such as in the Casablanca and Curicó Valleys. He has experimented with new clones and new varieties, such as Syrah and Sangiovese, and has sourced new sites in order to produce high-quality Chardonnays and Sauvignons. Importantly, Eduardo has developed a flagship wine, Don Maximiano Founder's Reserve, resolutely Bordeaux in style, 'to demonstrate our passion for quality'.

The current Viña Errázuriz portfolio comprises not only Viña Errázuriz and Viñedo Chadwick but also Viña Caliterra and Seña, both of which are joint projects with the Californian wine producer Robert Mondavi, who would never have lent his name and his expertise had he not believed in Chile's potential. Having seen the country's vineyards, however, and having been struck by how similar they were to the vineyards of the Napa Valley 30 years before (and having discovered how persuasive Eduardo could be), Mondavi quickly became involved. In 1996 he and Eduardo formed a fifty-fifty partnership to come up with a Chilean wine that would rival the top wines of the world.

The remarkable Cabernet-based wine Seña was launched in 1997 and hailed immediately as Chile's first serious wine of real quality. The Seña vineyard is in the Aconcagua Valley, and the wine is made at the Don Maximiano Estate under the guidance of Tim Mondavi, Robert's son, and winemaker Edward Flaherty, although a purpose-built winery is soon to be constructed.

'I believe that Seña has shown the world the potential of Chile as a wine region,' says Eduardo. 'It's been a dream to work with Mondavi, and his name has alerted the critics to Chile's potential, the proof of which is in the tasting of the wines.' Getting Mondavi on board was a shrewd move both financially and in terms of marketing, since his name is famous throughout the world for releasing California from its 'jug wine' image.

Eduardo's most personal project is Viñedo Chadwick, a top-class red wine created in memory of his late father, of which only 1,200

Above: Don Alfonso was one of Chile's finest polo players, and the locker room at Viñedo Chadwick, virtually untouched since his death in 1993, is lined with sepia-coloured team photographs and cluttered with the many trophies that he won.
Below: You are never too young to learn. Alejandra Chadwick gets up to speed with her wine-tasting techniques.
Opposite: The harvest under way at the Don Maximiano estate.

cases are made each year. The grapes come from a small vineyard planted around Eduardo's former family home, an outpost of calm surrounded by the rumbling, unprepossessing suburbs of Santiago. 'This is where I was born and where my father died in 1993,' he says. 'I wanted to create a wine that would represent my home and my heritage while also standing as a testament to my father. The vineyard was planted on my father's old polo field, and I feel that he would have approved – his twin passions were polo and wine, after all. And, conveniently, Viñedo Chadwick doesn't compete with our other wines because it comes from a completely different region.'

Having proved that his company could make wines of the highest quality, Eduardo began to concentrate on improving their marketing and distribution. Viña Errázuriz sells 90 per cent of its wines outside of Chile, and so in 1994 Eduardo joined forces with the celebrated Burgundy producer Louis Jadot to create Hatch Mansfield Agencies, a UK-based distribution house for Errázuriz and other fine wines. 'We regard the export market as our home market,' says Eduardo, 'with Europe accounting for some 70 per cent of our company's sales. The UK is by far our largest market, followed by Ireland, Denmark and Switzerland. It must be said, though,' he pauses with an ironic grin, 'that France, Italy and Spain are not key markets of ours.'

Eduardo is a proud man, proud of his ancient English lineage, proud of his Chilean nationality and proud of his four daughters, each of whom can twist him around their little fingers. But he has most reason to be proud of what he has achieved with Viña Errázuriz. The combination of an astute business sense and a love of wine has resulted in one of Chile's – and indeed, the wine world's – greatest success stories. Since taking over the company, Eduardo has revolutionized the winemaking equipment, caught consumers' interest by his alliance with Robert Mondavi, and ensured an efficient distribution through his partnership with Louis Jadot.

His spell in Oxford has given Eduardo a chance to ponder, to step back and get a clearer picture of what is required for his company to build on its success. 'Market share is all very well,' he says, 'but we're quality- not quantity-driven. We know that we make fine wine at Errázuriz, but we need to consolidate our image and reputation with our consumers. Since 1995 we've been refining and tweaking, all of which takes time. But if I've learned one thing, it is that you need to be patient as a winegrower – just as you need to be patient as the father of four girls!'

M Chapoutier

Rhône, France

Michel Chapoutier's diminutive stature belies his enormous presence, and to spend any time in his company is to be left breathless, as if buffeted by an intellectual whirlwind. A man of whizz-bang, dynamic energy, fuelled by an unbridled enthusiasm and an obsessive commitment to quality, Michel – although barely yet out of his thirties – has been at the helm of top-class Rhône producer M Chapoutier for 15 years.

The firm was founded in Tain l'Hermitage in the Rhône Valley in 1808 and has passed from father to son ever since, with Michel representing the seventh generation to run the company. Michel took outright control of his family's winery in 1990. Although a famous name in the Rhône and highly regarded internationally, Chapoutier was going through a lean time and was on the verge of bankruptcy. Michel bought out the rest of the family, with his grandfather, his father, his brother – and the bank – all selling their shares to him.

Although Michel is deeply fond of his family and proud of its heritage, he knew that to make a success of reviving Chapoutier he had to do it alone. 'With my brother Marc around I always felt that there were two drivers in the car,' he says. 'Members of one's family can be associates, workers or irritants and it is best, therefore, to be alone.'

The company owns some 210 hectares (519 acres) of vineyards and produces between 90 and 100 different wines each year, including those from such celebrated appellations as Hermitage, Crozes-Hermitage, St Joseph, Côte Rôtie, Condrieu, Châteauneuf-du-Pape and Banyuls. In addition to its own vineyards, Chapoutier supervises the vinification processes and, in some cases, the cultivation, of other appellation wines commercialized by the company, such as Cornas, Gigondas, Muscat de Beaumes-de-Venise, Côtes du Rhône, Tavel and Vins de Pays d'Oc. The company's total production each year is roughly 225,000 cases, of which about 60 per cent is exported.

Since taking over, Michel has made changes in the cellar and in the management structure, while developing new products and new wines, and the company is once again a major wine-producing force. Michel has bought additional vineyards – notably in Condrieu, St Joseph and Hermitage – as well as dipping a toe in the water of the New World with the purchase of four vineyards in South Australia. He has instigated innovations such as overprinting all his wine labels in Braille, setting up the M Chapoutier Wines and Health Association – a charity whose aim is to raise public awareness of bone marrow transplants – and creating a professional award for the best trainee sommelier in French wines and spirits. There are even plans to organize cultural activities associated with wine, including tourist trails through his vineyards with signs and information packs that would teach visitors how the vineyard links them with the history, the botany and the geology of the region.

'We cannot resist Michel's passions,' laughs Albéric Mazoyer, the general and technical manager at Chapoutier. 'He has made massive changes in the company, none of which, I believe, could have been put in place so quickly in a non-family company. It's true to say that the personality of our boss is reflected in our wines and we do make very forceful wines.'

But such changes are but a sideshow compared to the heart of the revolution undertaken by Michel for which he is best known: the adoption of biodynamic farming in all his vineyards – taking organic farming a step further. The principles of biodynamic farming were first set out in 1924 by Rudolf Steiner. Very simply, they involve the care of the soil by the use of organic, rather than synthetic, chemicals, and also by applying such products at specific times during the annual cycle, recognizing that the land is an organism in its own right.

Above and opposite: **Michel Chapoutier (above) intends to capitalize on his vineyards' past (opposite), encouraging customers not only to buy his wines, but also to ponder on their history. He believes that New World producers understand wine tourism far better than the French, who take the historical and cultural links with wine for granted. There will be tourist trails through the vines because, he says, 'We want to tell people that it's the vineyard that holds our history together.'**
Previous page: **The vineyards of Crozes-Hermitage and Hermitage are on precipitous terraces rising up some 100m (330ft) from the river, and the Chapoutier sign can be seen for miles around.**

'Our sole aim is to make great wines that please our customers,' says Michel. 'And if we can do that biodynamically, then so much the better, but our goal is not simply to make biodynamic wines. However, we need to go back to the earth and let the soil dictate, because great wines are made in the vineyards and not in the cellar. The winemaker must subordinate himself to the total *terroir* of his vineyard and let nature make the wine.'

'Michel's choice to go biodynamic was courageous,' argues Albéric. 'Of course, we all thought that he was crazy. It's not easy being a pioneer, and it helped that he was the sole decision-maker. But biodynamism is now so integrated into the spirit of the company, and we're so sure that it's good for the vines, that we know it must be good for us.'

Chapoutier might be innovative in terms of viticulture, but it is resolutely traditional when it comes to grape varieties – not too difficult since the Rhône and Roussillon regions permit more varieties to be grown than anywhere else in France. Michel favours unblended wines, believing that blending dilutes a wine's character – hence his 100 per cent Grenache Châteauneuf-du-Pape, for example. This is something of a New World attitude for a Frenchman to take, given that Châteauneuf-du-Pape is permitted to (and usually does) contain up to 13 different varieties.

Michel and his wife, Corinne, and their children, Maxim and Mathilde, live in a spectacular house – the earliest parts of which date from 1492 – perched on the edge of a hill overlooking the Rhône Valley. A former farm, the estate is still home to several chickens, ducks, geese and sheep, most of which are destined for the pot since both Michel and his wife are expert and enthusiastic cooks.

Cooking is just one of many topics about which Michel has a strong opinion, and an evening spent with him can be an exhilarating experience. The food and the wine will, of course, be of the highest quality and the conversation, or rather lecture, will scorch across a thousand seemingly unrelated topics. Without prompting, he will launch into a dissertation on whatever subject manages to elbow its way to the front of his overcrowded brain and, just for good measure, will pepper such soliloquies with Wildean bons mots. 'To ask the alcoholic strength of a wine is as rude as asking a lady her age,' he will say in a voice laden with mock gravitas, before beginning a discursive monologue on overly alcoholic wines.

Half-drunk glasses of wine will be emptied over the terrace as Michel's impatience to crack open another bottle gets the better of him. All the while opinions on such diverse topics as the Bible, classical music, French poets, rugby or the merits of British beef continue to tumble forth. And he is nothing

Right and below: Michel Chapoutier in typically exuberant mood surrounded by his family and the inevitable open bottles and glasses of wine with which he regularly educates his young children.

if not dogmatic. 'Good beef depends on the grass,' he will declare in a voice that brooks no argument. 'Good, tasty grass equals good, tasty beef. Therefore the best beef comes from rainy countries, such as Britain, Ireland, Germany and Denmark. The Burgundians make me laugh; their beef *is* tender, but it isn't tasty like British beef.' He looks at you as if challenging you to disagree. This leads to a survey of British cooking habits and a mini lecture on food in general. 'In Britain, the raw ingredients are among the best in the world – but everything is boiled. It's because of the weather. You used not to be able to keep the meat long, so it had to be boiled. Boiled beef, boiled mutton and boiled bacon. In France, however…'

All one does is light his cerebral touchpaper and retire to watch the explosions as his prejudices and opinions – well informed and reasoned – flood out. Michel is enthusiasm personified, and all his comments and discussions are punctuated by pauses as he takes time to conduct the CD of Saint-Saëns's Organ Symphony, which is booming out over the valley at full volume.

Michel loves music, any music, from Mozart to Le Hot Club de France to the Rolling Stones. 'My father would never let me listen to music. But I love it, not least because it is available to all. Everyone is free to listen to music and it doesn't depend on wealth. I want to do the same for wine. To make a good £200 bottle of wine is easy. To make a good £7 bottle is the test,' he says. And he is as fond of art as he is of music, and his home and office are full of modern pieces. Poetry too, is a passion.

'Of course, Baudelaire is my favourite poet. I'm definitely a Baudelaire man, not a Verlaine man. I like poets who ask "are you bad and happy to be bad?" not "are you bad and sad to be bad?" One day I plan to make a wine with a poem on the back label with the title of the poem as the name of the wine. One of Baudelaire's poems would be ideal.'

But Michel's opinions aren't always random. He is always thinking about how to improve the company and its wines. 'Michel hardly ever sleeps,' explains Yann Pinot, the Chapoutier shop manager. 'He comes into the office in the mornings saying, "I've had an idea!" And we all say, "Uh-oh!"'

He is not without humour; on being asked what his current idea is, Michel replies with a guffaw, 'My current idea is that my wife is so useful to me, that if I had three wives, I'd be three times as rich.' He even makes fun of his own dogmatism. 'With food,' he says, 'I'm very intolerant, and anyone who asks for a blue steak rather than a well-done one scores points with me. I wanted to write in our staff canteen, "No entry for the Taliban or Vegetarians".'

Michel is clearly something of an egalitarian, both in his personal views, but also in company practices, and he has a very sensitive and human approach to life. All the 120 permanent employees and 30–40 seasonal staff, as well as Michel and Corinne, eat in the staff refectory. It is simple and homely and more like a kitchen in someone's house than a factory canteen. Bottles of wine and flagons of water line the tables and, alongside a help-yourself buffet of cold meats and salad, there is always a hot dish, often decided by Michel himself. 'Food is too important to delegate,' he exclaims. 'When I take charge of the menus, my employees know that they will eat well. And well-fed employees are happy employees!'

Michel's left-leaning philosophy is no affectation – he holds his beliefs sincerely and they inform his business life as much as his personal one. For a romantic and a dreamer, Michel is remarkably practical, and he has proved that poets can make efficient businessmen. 'We can make a big profit when we make an outstanding wine – but to interest future drinkers, we must make our basic wine without making a profit, and all our lowest price wines at Chapoutier are sold without making any profit. You could say that they are our samples. We want people to discover them and to graduate to our other wines. There's too much snobbery in wine and I'd like to see the back of it. I want people to enjoy wine and to prove that one doesn't have to be a money lover to be a wine lover.'

Michel is still young, and it will be fascinating to watch his company's progress over the next decade or so. Where will his ideas take Chapoutier next? 'Michel has been hugely innovative,' says Albéric Mazoyer, 'but his blood and genetics are traditional and hark back to the family's history. He has been a new brush, but only to polish the jewel that was already here.'

Above and opposite: Maison Chapoutier is a well-balanced blend of tradition and innovation. The wines might be made in customary Rhône style, but the labels (opposite, top left) are overwritten in Braille and the vineyards (bottom) are run biodynamically. Biodynamism was first of all an agronomic choice – it was good for the land. Now the system is so closely associated with the company, biodynamism is also good for the brand. And as Michel points out, if one nurtures the land, the land will produce better grapes, which means better wines, which means higher profits.

Château Climens

Bordeaux (Sauternes-Barsac), France

'**Y**ou could say that wine is in our blood,' laughs Bérénice Lurton-Thomas as she sits at dinner, surrounded by her nine brothers and sisters, all of whom, remarkably enough, own chateaux in Bordeaux. It is a noisy occasion, and the laughter and leg-pulling are interspersed by the important business of catching up with the news of each other's estates, amid gentle displays of sibling rivalry.

Below: 'Running both the Climens and de Camarsac estates is hard,' says Bérénice, 'but it's a great life and I do it because I love it.'
Opposite: Château de Camarsac's elegant dovecote stands proudly amid the estate's 60 hectares (148 acres) of vines.
Previous page: The courtyard cottage at Bérénice Lurton's second estate, the 12th-century Ch de Camarsac, is home to her and her husband, Laurent Thomas.

Bérénice, the youngest of the ten siblings, was barely out of university when, in 1992, her father, Lucien Lurton, divided up his many winemaking properties among his children. Bérénice was not only given the little-known estate Ch de Camarsac, but was also given a half share, with her sister Brigitte, in an absolute peach of a property – the Premier Cru Classé Ch Climens, a small chateau in Sauternes-Barsac famed for its sublime sweet wines.

'At first I didn't want the estates,' she now admits. 'After all, I was only 22 and I wasn't at all sure that this was what I wanted my destiny to be. But after a while I realized what an amazing challenge it would be, and I found that I couldn't refuse such an opportunity.'

Within a few months of assuming control of Ch Climens, however, Brigitte and Bérénice realized that there could be only one captain of the ship, and although they have remained close as sisters, it was clear that they were never going to be able to work together harmoniously. As a result, Bérénice bought out her sister's interest in the property and she has remained in sole charge ever since, representing only the fifth family to own the estate since its foundation in the 16th century. In the 11 years since taking control of Ch Climens, Bérénice has gained a formidable reputation for the skill with which she has turned a celebrated, but nevertheless underachieving, chateau into one that produces sweet wines of the highest possible quality.

Sauternes-Barsac is a small commune in the Gironde, south-east of Bordeaux, and it is here that some of the world's finest sweet wines are made, the most famous of which is Ch d'Yquem. Producing sweet wines of such quality is a complex and laborious business. The wines are made from grapes affected by noble rot, the name given to *botrytis cinerea* – known in France as *pourriture noble*. Botrytis is a mould that, in areas blessed with sun and humid and misty conditions, attacks certain grapes, making them shrivel and rot, thus concentrating their sugar and flavour. The grapes are picked individually by hand and produce wines high both in alcohol and richness of flavour. It is a hugely wasteful process however, for while a single vine is capable of producing one bottle of ordinary wine, it will produce only one glass of Sauternes-Barsac. And for botrytis to work well, conditions must be perfect; and so it is that in some years (1984, 1987, 1992 and 1993, for example) Ch Climens has produced no wine at all.

'Everything at Ch Climens is very basic,' says Bérénice. 'We have basic vinification, not because we insist on tradition, but because we don't need state-of-the-art equipment. Concentration and purity together is the key to our wine, and for that a perfect harvest is vital. If it goes wrong there, it doesn't matter how good our skills of vinification are, or our cellar work, the wine just won't work.'

It goes without saying that poor grapes lead inevitably to poor wine, but in many other wine regions the careful blending of different grape varieties – especially when one variety fails at harvest time – or sleight of hand in the winery can salvage a bad vintage.

'Our reputation here is for purity, and I won't allow standards in the vineyard to harm this,' says Bérénice. Each year, 30 or so highly skilled Portuguese pickers come to do the harvest, and Bérénice values them greatly. She has built a house for them to use and she pays both their wages and their travel expenses. Each picker has his or her own numbered bucket and his or her own numbered row

of vines to pick. It is strictly controlled and Bérénice doesn't allow her pickers to work elsewhere in the region, for fear that they might absorb different working habits and practices. 'If these Portuguese leave me, or if I can't get the right people to do our harvest, I'll give up!' she declares.

Unlike almost all the other wines in Sauternes-Barsac, Ch Climens is made solely from Sémillon, rather than being a blend of that grape and Sauvignon Blanc – with a possible dash of Muscadelle. 'Sémillon is a demanding grape, but it's a great translator of *terroir*,' says Bérénice. The difficulty for Bérénice lies in the blending of the different lots that come in from the vineyard, and getting the balance of ageing and freshness just right – all from this one grape variety. The lots comprise juice from the grapes picked from different parts of the vineyard on different days, with the use of different types of oak barrels adding another dimension to the equation.

'Our wine's complexity is often remarked upon,' says Bérénice, 'but it comes from the marriage of one grape with one soil. We take a long time to get our blend right each year, and we're often the last chateau to present its wines. There's always a freshness to Climens and it's powerful in a light and elegant way. Other producers say that they use Sauvignon for freshness, and I laugh because I get all the freshness I need from Sémillon.'

Five people are involved in this delicate task of blending the wines: the consultant oenologists Lucien Llorca and Pierre Sudraud, the *maître de chai* Christian Broustaut (who has been at Ch Climens for 30 years), the technical director Frédéric Nivelle, and Bérénice herself. 'Blends have to be better than the sum of the lots that go into it,' explains Bérénice. 'What we're looking for is dynamism, brightness, elegance and élan. I believe that with blending, we're not creating it, we're discovering it. It's like a treasure hunt and sometimes I fear that we'll never discover the perfect blend.'

Bérénice is bound by the strictest of wine laws that govern which grapes she is entitled to grow and in what manner she might grow them. This is in contrast to the producers of the New World, of course, where producers can grow more or less what they want, where they want and how they

Left: Bérénice prefers to live at Ch de Camarsac rather than Ch Climens, and with a great deal of renovation still to do, it must be useful to have an architect for a husband. **Below:** The grape pickers at Ch Climens are highly skilled, and each picker is allocated his own particular numbered bucket into which the hand-picked grapes – not bunches – are placed, one by one.

want. But Bérénice was born to the business – unlike many a New World winemaker, who might be a retired accountant or dentist – being almost as much a product of the local *terroir* as her wines. Far from simply being an idle custodian of the estate, she has proved that even in this most traditional of wine regions, someone with dynamism, energy and skill will have an immense effect on the wine they produce. The whole set-up at Ch Climens is the very antithesis of the New World with the size and shape of the 29-hectare (74-acre) estate having scarcely changed in centuries.

The Lurton family is one of the most influential winegrowing families in the region (and an increasing influence in the New World, too), owning or managing some of the finest chateaux in Bordeaux. Bérénice's father Lucien lives at Ch Brane-Cantenac, and her uncle André is the largest single owner – in terms of hectares – in the Gironde; Ch La Louvière, among others, belongs to him. Bérénice's five brothers and four sisters own countless other properties, including Ch Bouscaut, Ch Desmirail, Ch Doisy-Dubroca, Ch Dufort-Vivens and Ch Duplessis. Oh, and just for good measure, her first cousin Pierre is the manager of Ch Cheval Blanc.

'None of us in the family is arrogant,' says Bérénice. 'It's not who we are but what we're doing with what we've got. We're serving the land and our estates, which have histories and traditions that we respect. We want to make them live and to put our print on them in a certain way, but not too much. Although all of us ten siblings are very different in character, we all have respect. Our life was always very simple and we weren't rich kids with fast cars. We were given responsibility with our estates and those that haven't gone into managing them have pretty serious and useful jobs.'

The dynasty started with Léonce Récapet (1858–1943), who made a fortune thanks to his distillery in the Entre-Deux-Mers. As his wealth accumulated, so he bought vineyards and wine estates in and around Bordeaux, including, in the 1920s, Ch Brane-Cantenac, along with a share in the famed Ch Margaux – later swapped for Ch Clos Fourtet in St Emilion. Léonce's daughter married François Lurton, with whom she had a daughter, Simone, and three sons, André, Lucien and Dominique, who inherited these and several other estates.

André's two sons, Jacques and François, have winemaking interests in Argentina and Spain, trading under the name Bodegas J & F Lurton; Dominique's two sons, Pierre and Marc, manage Ch Cheval Blanc and own Ch Reynier in the Entre-Deux-Mers respectively, while Lucien's children, well, they own rather a lot. It had long been Lucien's intention to settle which of his many offspring was going to inherit which of

Above: The name Climens first appeared on a contract dated 1547, and the estate's 29-hectare (74-acre) vineyard has remained practically unchanged in size and shape since its creation.

Opposite: Despite its fame, everything at Ch Climens is kept simple and unassuming. Even the 18th-century chartreuse-style chateau itself is low key, with its understated architecture. 'They only added the towers so that they could call it a chateau,' giggles Bérénice.

his many chateaux and so, in 1992, he invited them all to a family meeting at Ch Bouscaut. His original idea had been that each of them should draw lots to decide the issue, but his son Gonzague persuaded him that it would be fairer if everyone were allowed to choose the property they wanted. Each was allowed to make three choices, subject to certain stipulations that Lucien made.

Originally, only two of the ten children – Henri and Marie-Laure – were involved in wine. Denis was a lawyer studying to be an actor, Bérénice was at university studying politics, Sophie was working as a translator in Rome, Gonzague was working in a bank (but pining to make wine), Brigitte was travelling, Louis was a lawyer (but also helping run two of the family estates), Thierry was a social worker and Edwige a teacher. But when Lucien made his plans known to his children, some hurriedly took crash-courses in wine lore from Henri, while others decided to continue in their chosen careers and to employ managers and winemakers, or to leave their siblings to run things.

Remarkably, each of the children got more or less the property that they had chosen, and there were no tears and no squabbling that day at Ch Bouscaut, although Bérénice's sister Sophie jokes, 'All the girls wanted Ch de Camarsac because it is so pretty.'

In fact, so beguiling did Bérénice find the 12th-century chateau at Camarsac, with its 60 hectares (148 acres) of vineyards, that she and her husband Laurent Thomas – an architect and archaeologist – have made it their home. Not only that, she hopes to raise the profile of the property's wines when she launches a new label from the estate: Le Prince Noir. 'My father thought it was impossible to achieve anything there,' she says, 'and I like to think that I've proved him wrong. We're making good wine, and are going to make better wine, albeit while losing pots of money.'

Although she is rightly proud of what she is on the verge of achieving at Ch de Camarsac, Bérénice's main priority is clearly to maintain the progress that she has made in rehabilitating the reputation of Ch Climens. Bérénice dislikes its wine being described as pudding or dessert wine. She is keen on food and wine matching, and believes that Ch Climens is extremely adaptable – more so than it is often given credit for – working well as an aperitif or as an accompaniment to poultry and veal dishes, mushrooms and spiced food. 'Ch Climens is discreet,' she argues, 'and I want its wines to be bought for their quality, not to impress like a Rolex watch. There is still much work to be done here but, as for the future, I don't like to look too far ahead; only as far as the next vintage.'

Domaine Daniel-Etienne Defaix

Chablis, France

Daniel-Etienne Defaix is a big bear of a man, possessed of a bone-crunching handshake and an infectious giggle that rumbles deep within him before exploding into a loud wheezy laugh. Despite admitting to too much rich food (especially oysters and foie gras), too many cigars, too little exercise and too little sleep, he glows with health and vitality, his eyes sparkling as he talks of his many passions, the greatest of which, of course, is his wine.

Above: **Daniel-Etienne with his late father, Etienne, and son, Paul-Etienne.**

Opposite: **The company's average annual production is 170,000 bottles, although in a good year this can rise to 200,000. Daniel used to do all his harvesting by hand until he decided to invest in a pair of picking machines. 'It's an expensive method,' he says, 'but the machine is best, although it took me too long to realize this. It helps me make a good vintage in a bad year. You need a good driver with good eyes, though!'**

Previous page: **Looking towards the town of Chablis from the estate.**

Daniel began his life as a winemaker in the face of much opposition from his father, Etienne, even though 14 generations of his family had been in the business before him. At only 18 and having just started at university, Daniel was offered 1.5 prime hectares (4 acres) in the Premier Cru Le Lys vineyard, an opportunity that he felt too exciting to miss. After all, his father, his grandfather (Maurice) and two of his uncles (Jean and Bernard) were winemakers, so why shouldn't he join in, too?

Even at such a young age, Daniel believed in the value of old-fashioned winemaking and looked to his traditionally minded grandfather as a model, rather than his father, who simply churned out as much as he could as quickly as he could, selling all that he produced to wine giant Nicolas. Daniel decided to be rigorously traditional in his methods, a philosophy that he has maintained ever since.

'I asked my father for his help in buying the vineyards,' says Daniel, 'but he refused because he said that making wine like my grandfather would keep me a poor man for life, whereas making wine like he did would make me rich. I'm a crazy man and a stubborn one, and I told him that one doesn't need to eat bread every day. So I went to the bank and bought the vineyard, even though my studies didn't finish until I was 22. My father neither helped in terms of money nor in terms of equipment or employees. I loved him, of course, but I have to say that I am where I am today despite him.'

Daniel travelled home between lectures and seminars to tend his vines and after three years he had something to show for his efforts. His methods have barely changed over the years. He picks only the very ripest grapes, with the elimination, grape by grape, of unripe or rotten ones. Vinification starts with a slow pressing for three hours followed by 18 hours of natural settling of the must. A three-week alcoholic fermentation at low temperature, using only natural yeast, is followed by a malo-lactic fermentation. Most importantly, and alone among Chablis producers, Daniel insists on the ancient practice of *bâtonnage*, which is the systematic stirring of the lees every month for 18 months which, he believes, leads to fuller-flavoured and more richly structured wines. 'Two generations ago, all of Chablis was produced with *bâtonnage*,' he says, 'but time is money and the banks don't like us using it.' He only uses oak for his Grand Cru and then only for a third of the wines, because he doesn't want to mask the flavour lent by the soil or the microclimate. 'These vineyards are 1,000 years old – why hide their history?' he asks.

Despite Daniel's success, Etienne continued to keep his distance, and it wasn't until 1995 that he conceded defeat. 'My father was amazed that I had succeeded,' says Daniel. 'And he finally came to congratulate me, although he still didn't approve of my methods, thinking that each year I was taking too high a risk. Eventually, though, he realized that I was paying six times more tax than he was and that I'd paid off the bank. He then said that he was proud of me and that by not helping me, he *had* helped me. And he was right: he made me prove myself and prove that I could succeed.'

In September of that year, Etienne suggested merging his own vineyard with that of his son, whom he agreed could oversee the winemaking. Etienne ceased to supply Nicolas and the wines of the combined 26 hectares (64 acres) were sold either under the name of Etienne Defaix or Daniel-Etienne Defaix. Etienne has since died, and today Daniel owns the whole estate.

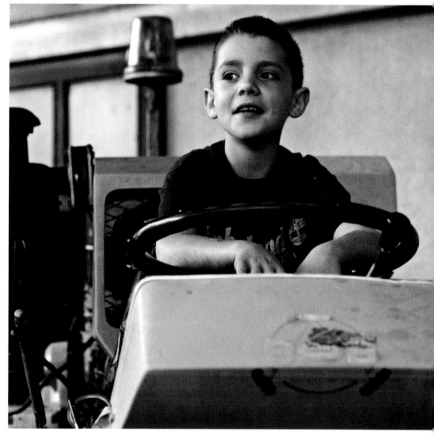

This page: **The distinctive church of Chablis seen from Domaine Daniel-Etienne Defaix's Premier Cru vineyard, Le Lys.**

Outside France and the UK, Daniel's wines are sold mainly in the United States, Norway, Belgium, Hong Kong, Japan, Italy and South Africa. He refuses to sell to supermarkets and concentrates instead on selling to restaurants, which accounts for about three-quarters of his sales. He supplies over 500 restaurants in France and it is his proud boast that, unlike any other Chablis producer, he sells his wine to every Michelin-starred restaurant in the UK. His policy of ageing his wines before releasing them means that restaurants are in a position to offer fully mature wines to their patrons.

'I do no publicity and no advertising,' he says. 'I have fax and e-mail, and the orders just flood in, even though I don't do any promotion. I will make an enormous effort for my customers, and they are incredibly loyal to me, as I am loyal to them. We stick together.'

Daniel believes that his wines represent good value, given the amount of work that goes into making them. 'My wines are expensive and so drinking them must be a great pleasure – not a medium pleasure. Also, the morning after drinking my wine you wake up and say, "What a wonderful day it is!", even though it's raining. That's the mark of a great wine – great pleasure and great health.'

Daniel's success as a winemaker has allowed him to develop many other interests in and around Chablis, and he has proved himself to be an astute businessman. 'I'm alone in what I do,' he says. 'My father never helped me and my wife, Fabienne, although incredibly supportive, isn't involved in what I do. She always says the same thing when I come up with a project: "Is it feasible and are you capable?"'

In 1986 he opened the first wine shop in Chablis, a resource that had hitherto been surprisingly absent. It was a phenomenal success. 'I didn't make money as a result. I made gold!' he exclaims. His rivals cottoned on quickly and within five years there were more than 25 wine shops in the town. Not a bad thing, Daniel reckons, as it helps promote the area. With this in mind, he gathered together 15 other Chablis producers to set up a hotel and restaurant in the town called Hostellerie des Clos, while also involving himself in other similar establishments. 'If I don't do this, someone else will, and I'll get my throat cut,' he explains.

In addition to his role as restaurateur and hotelier, Daniel is an accomplished property developer. Not only has he restored the beautiful old chateau in the hamlet of Milly – just outside Chablis – in which he lives with his wife and children, Paul-Etienne (8) and Anne-Claire (13), he has also been renovating a dozen or so houses in the centre of town. The courtyard around which these stand will be let out for exhibitions, concerts, dinners, parties and tastings, while the houses themselves will be used as accommodation for his proposed wine tours. This development has so far taken 13 years. 'It's been like Ancient Egypt or Ancient Greece with all the work that has been going on,' he sighs.

He has renovated the 1,000 year-old cellars beneath the buildings, which will also be used for events, especially concerts. 'Roman cellars are perfect acoustically, I've found, unlike Gothic cellars where there's too much echo. It has taken me so long to restore the cellars and the roofs of my buildings that it will fall to my children to look after the in-betweens.'

Daniel enjoys listing the several 'records' he holds. His vineyards are the oldest in Chablis (about 1,000 years old), as are his vines (about 50 years old on average). He uses the oldest winemaking techniques in the region, owns the oldest chateau and is the last producer to make red wine here. He opened the first wine shop in Chablis, was the first producer to have a website, and his property development company makes him the largest single property owner in Chablis.

'What gets me up in the mornings is my wine. It is my passion, whereas my property deals and other activities are my "amusements". Although my wines are expensive, I make only a small profit. I can afford to do what I do because of customer loyalty and because I don't take holidays and I don't have a house in Switzerland or a yacht in the Mediterranean. For almost 20 years I have lived like a poor man, although I am NOT a poor man! If I sold up tomorrow, I'd be the richest man in Chablis. But everything that I've done, I've done for my wine. I'm so happy that people like what I do and like my wines. This is enough for me.'

Domaine Faiveley

Burgundy, France

François Faiveley's family has lived in Burgundy since before the French Revolution, although François himself belies the Burgundian stereotype by being tall, angular and remarkably slender. He glows with a healthy tan, thanks to regular jaunts on his yacht, *Glenn*, but fails to present a relaxed air because of his frantic gum-chewing – taken up since he stopped smoking.

François's day job is chairman, CEO and controlling shareholder of Faiveley Industries, a public-listed company with annual gross sales of around £250m. It is one of the world's largest engineering companies, with factories in France, Spain, Germany, China and Brazil, producing anything from air-conditioning units and goods for the textile industry to scent bottles and the automatic doors on France's celebrated TGVs.

Hugely successful though this company is, it doesn't represent François's real passion. What makes his blood race – that is, apart from sailing and music – is Domaine Joseph Faiveley, his family wine company, famed for its sublime burgundies. François confesses that many of his colleagues at Faiveley Industries think his love of winemaking very odd, while as many of his colleagues at Domaine Faiveley believe that to earn one's living as an industrialist is nothing short of bizarre. François himself is in no doubt about his priorities. 'On my passport, and in my heart, I am a winemaker,' he says, 'not an industrialist nor an engineer. In Faiveley Industries we make spare parts and never see the whole picture: it must be so dull to work on an assembly line just doing bits and pieces here and there. But winemaking is so satisfying intellectually. I love wine, because it is one of the few worlds where one sees everything from beginning to end, and where one has control at every step, from planting the grape to choosing which type of capsule to put on the bottle.'

Domaine Joseph Faiveley was founded in 1825 by Pierre Faiveley, and François is the sixth generation of his family to own and run it. (His parents met at a conference when, thanks to an alphabetical seating plan and the fact that they shared a surname, although they were not related, they found themselves placed next to one another.) François's elder brother, Thierry, had no passion either for wine or for engineering and chose to forge a career as a painter, so it fell to François to join the family firms. He began to take over from his father in 1976 (when he was only 25) and assumed total control in 1978.

The company is based in Nuits-St-Georges, where modern offices sit atop a warren of cellars, which were built in around 1800. Copied from the Lanson cellars in Champagne, they were originally used for producing and storing sparkling burgundy. About 100 people work in the company, including a handful of staff to manage the company's other cellars in Mercurey, although, as François puts it, 'The aristocracy of our wines is fermented in Nuits-St-Georges.'

The company is one of the largest owners of vineyards in Burgundy, boasting the highest percentage of Grand Cru and Premier Cru vineyards of any producer in the region: 70 hectares (173 acres) in Mercurey and 45 hectares (111 acres) in the Côte d'Or. The vast majority of the company's grapes come from their own vineyards; the rest, used mainly for generic wines such as Beaujolais and Mâcon, are bought in from the multitude of small growers that abound in Burgundy. Each year about 80,000 cases – 60,000 from their own vineyards and 20,000 in their role as a *négociant* – of around 45 different wines are produced with all the great names of the region represented: Chablis, Meursault, Chassagne-Montrachet, Puligny-Montrachet, Corton Charlemagne, Santenay, Volnay, Vosne-Romanée, Morey-St-Denis, Gevrey-Chambertin, Echézeaux, Clos de Vougeot, Chambolle-Musigny and Nuits-St-Georges.

François oversees all the vinification and is very particular in his methods, although he is adamant that 'there's no secret to winemaking, that's the secret. It's all about good practices, hard work, good land and fine weather. One needs to be as good a gardener as one is a winemaker.'

He believes firmly that fine wine is made in the vineyard and that the quality of the grapes is the key. 'Only in fairy tales does the ugly frog turn into the handsome prince,' he says. 'Not in wine! Bad practices and bad grapes lead to bad wine. There's no mystery.'

Opposite: The chateau at Clos de Vougeot; here the Faiveleys own 1.29 precious hectares (3.18 acres) of vineyard.

Below: François and Anne Faiveley with their daughter, Eve, the first girl to be born into the Faiveley family since 1772 – hence her name.

Previous page: From the outset, the Faiveley family realized that the best way to guarantee quality was to control the source of supply by owning and managing a large estate. The greater part of the family resources was therefore devoted to acquiring vines in the best villages, and today the company owns a total of about 120 hectares (300 acres) of vineyards in prime sites, such as here at Grand Cru Clos de Vougeot.

Yields are kept to a minimum and the use of fertilizer is forbidden, except where there is a deficiency, and then only organic fertilizer is used. All the grapes are hand-picked and sorted by hand. 'All I say to the pickers is, "If you see a grape, pick it. We'll take care of the rest"', says François.

No artificial yeast is used either. 'Despite what they teach students at universities these days,' sniffs François, 'I just can't see the point of adding flavour-imparting yeasts when we've taken the trouble to keep the grapes from each parcel in the vineyards separate.'

The company prides itself on the fact that its wines age well, so vatting times are long and temperatures low. Temperature control is vital in François's view in order to help the wine keep its aromatic complexity. 'Your food will be cooked whether you blast it in a microwave for two minutes or simmer it on a cooker for two hours, but one will smell far more appetizing and enticing. The same is true with wine. The aroma is not for the winemaker but for the customer, and I ensure that we retain this by using cool fermentation.'

All the wines are put in oak and the company employs a full-time cooper. 'But I don't want to make New World wine,' says François, 'so we don't use that much.' The Grands Crus and most of the Premiers Crus (about 60,000 bottles in all) are bottled by hand from the barrel without filtering, while the rest of the production is bottled by machine, but rarely filtered or fined.

Just over half of Domaine Faiveley's wines are sold in France, with the rest being exported to over 40 countries, chiefly the UK, Japan and Switzerland. François is confident that there will always be a market for top-quality burgundies such as his, and the finest champagnes and clarets.

'There'll always be a place for the Grands Crus of France because they age so well, and because of their subtle evocation of *terroir*,' claims François. 'If we change simply to compete with the New World, we've lost the battle. The only way for us to compete is to produce wines of greater and greater quality. An American winemaker told me that in France we used the mystery of *terroir* to justify our prices. I replied that in the Napa Valley there's a classification by cheque book – the best sites on the slopes fetch more money.'

François is related to the Lurton family of Bordeaux, so when not drinking his own wines he'll drink claret. He also enjoys choosing wine from further afield to see what's going on elsewhere. 'It's important to compare,' he says, 'and foolish to stick to one's own wine all the time.' And when he isn't making wine or automatic sliding doors, François likes nothing more than to go out on his yacht. 'I simply adore sailing,' he says. 'To stand alone at the helm at night staring at the stars is, well, it's wonderful. My wife enjoys sailing, too, so long as we're at anchor all day.'

His other passion is music, about which he is immensely knowledgeable. Bach is a particular favourite of his, while the musician that he admires most is the Canadian pianist Glenn Gould, after whom he has named his yacht.

François spends about one-third of his time in Paris and two-thirds in Nuits-St-Georges, where the wine company is based. 'I can't bear to be in Paris more than one day a week,' he says with a grimace. 'The place has become a madhouse. I used to love going to Paris for concerts and so on. But no more, because once I'm in Paris I have only one passion and that is to get back to Burgundy.'

François and his Anglo-French wife, Anne, have two sons, Benoit and Erwan, and a daughter, Eve. Erwan, who has just returned from a year spent working in Philadelphia, is the one who has expressed the most interest in joining the family wine firm.

'I want him to work outside the wine world for at least a couple of years,' explains François. 'I've told the children not to do what Daddy does if they don't want to. I'd hate them to make bad wine. I'd far rather sell the company and give them the money. It wouldn't be the happiest day of my life, for sure, but nor would it be the worst. It's life!'

Opposite: François (top left) has a dryly witty sense of humour and can turn on an engaging, boyish charm, although he is equally likely to appear withdrawn and distracted, covering up conversational longueurs by humming to himself. His winemaking philosophy is simple: 'Growing grapes is like growing any fruit. People sometimes forget that the grape is a fruit, just as a cherry or a peach is. The grapes are everything; and good grapes, good *terroir* and good restricted yields equal good wine.'

Below: Faiveley: a name to reckon with in Burgundy since 1825.

Châteaux Langoa
and Léoville Barton

Bordeaux (St Julien), France

Anthony Barton, who pronounces his surname the English way, but the name of his wine the French way, couldn't be more English. Educated at Stowe and Jesus College, Cambridge (where he admits to doing little more than 'rowing and having tea'), and a member of the Turf Club, Anthony has the easy charm, self-deprecating humour, striking good looks and beautiful tailoring that are the hallmarks of the typical English gentleman.

Below: Anthony and Eva Barton with their daughter, Lillian, who has recently taken over from her father as the owner of the estates. Opposite: When the original Léoville estate was divided into three in 1821, Léoville Poyferré and Léoville Lascases both got chateaux, but Léoville Barton missed out. As a result, Langoa's chateau serves them both. Previous page: The exquisite Ch Langoa, which was built in the 1750s, is where the wines of both Langoa Barton and Léoville Barton are produced.

Except, of course, that he isn't English at all, 'No, I'm neither English nor French,' he explains. 'In fact, I'm not sure what I am, other than a square peg in a round hole. But having spent the first 20 years of my life in Ireland, where I was born, and the remaining 50 years in France, I'm usually described as a Bog-Frog.' When pressed, though, Anthony admits to a beating Irish heart when it comes to that crucial test of national identity – watching international rugby.

Now 73 – although he doesn't look it – Anthony is the eighth generation of his family to be involved in the Bordeaux wine trade. He started his career in the family firm of Barton & Guestier (now owned by Diageo), before taking over the estates at Langoa and Léoville from his uncle, Ronald, in 1983.

The Bartons' link with Bordeaux stretches back to Thomas Barton – known as 'French Tom' – who left his native Ireland in 1722 to work for two of his uncles who were trading in France (albeit not in wine). Thomas subsequently set up as a *negoçiant* and shipper by founding what later became Barton & Guestier. Despite the success of this venture and the wealth that it brought him, Thomas never took the logical step of buying vineyards in the region, owing to a law of the time – known as '*Le Droit d'Aubaine*' – which required that the estates of any foreigner who died in France should revert to the French Crown.

It was left to Thomas's grandson, Hugh, to become the first Barton to own an estate in Bordeaux when, in 1821, he bought Ch Langoa, in the heart of St Julien ('*Le Droit d'Aubaine*' having been abolished). He added to this a part of Ch Léoville, when this vast neighbouring estate was divided up and sold, his portion becoming known as Ch Léoville Barton – the two other (unequal) thirds becoming Ch Léoville Poyferré and Ch Léoville Lascases. Hugh also bought an estate in County Kildare in Ireland where he built Straffan House, which became home to the Barton family and where Anthony was later born and brought up. The next three generations of Hugh's descendents chose to remain in Ireland rather than in France, and it wasn't until Ronald inherited the Bordeaux vineyards in 1927 that a Barton once again made his home in the beautiful chateau at Langoa.

Although he had been engaged five times (entanglements that he never had the heart to break off, leaving that task to Anthony's mother), Ronald was a bachelor, and it was expected that Anthony would one day inherit the vineyards while his elder brother Christopher took over the family's Irish estates. However, when Straffan House had to be sold (it is now a country house hotel and golf club), Christopher was offered the Bordeaux estates as an alternative inheritance. But the vineyards had fallen into a parlous state and he turned them down, only to find that when Ronald dropped increasingly broad hints that they were Anthony's for the asking, Anthony declined them, too. As Anthony admits, the trouble was that he

Left and above: Anthony and Eva live in some splendour at Ch Langoa, while their daughter, Lillian, and her family live nearby in another house on the estate.

didn't know what he wanted to do with his life – other than hunt, shoot and fish. 'And just how would you finance such a life?' demanded his father. After trying, not very hard, to find a job, as a last resort Anthony agreed to go to Bordeaux to learn the trade preparatory to taking over the estates.

When he first arrived in France, Anthony spoke no French and knew nothing about wine. He was given a job at Barton & Guestier and tried to absorb as much about the subject as he could. 'I soon realized that I had not inherited an infallible palate but thought I could convince people of the contrary. I noticed that all the so-called experts could spit far and tidily, so I taught myself to spit in my bath, aiming at my big toe. I doubt I fooled many people,' Anthony recalls. 'In fact, I doubt I fooled anyone at all.' Since then, of course, Anthony has become one of the most respected figures in all Bordeaux.

He quickly learnt French from the family he lodged with in Bordeaux. Ronald paid for these digs but, apart from a small allowance from his grandmother, Anthony had no money to speak of. 'Uncle Ronald had no idea about money,' says Anthony. 'I had to work for two years at Barton & Guestier without getting paid. I suppose that it was that generation's view: "When I die, it's all yours, but until then you can just get on with it." I also told Ronald that I had been born on a farm and would far rather work at the chateau than in some office in Bordeaux, but he just said, "The chateau is where we lose money, Bordeaux is where we make money."'

There were consolations for Anthony during this sojourn in Bordeaux, however, because it was during this time that he met his Danish wife, Eva, who was also in France to learn the language. They married in 1955 and lived in very simple circumstances in Bordeaux before moving to a wing

Above: Anthony believes in continuity and his employees are well looked after, enjoying excellent meals in the chateau's *réfectoire*. Opposite: In the 1855 Classification, Ch Langoa was deemed a Third Growth and Ch Léoville a Second, but Anthony dismisses the idea of a re-evaluation. 'It will never happen. Of course it's out of date, but it's a historical document. There is an argument for changing it, but I'm against war of any kind, especially civil war.' Anthony has been involved in over 50 vintages at Langoa and Léoville, but is hardly one to sit back and admire the view. Improvements are constantly being made, and in 1990 he oversaw the construction of a new bottling line as well as a new *chai*, which can hold some 1,600 barrels.

of the chateau at Langoa in 1960, while Ronald continued to inhabit the main part. Then, in 1962 and completely out of the blue, Ronald, at the age of 60, decided to get married, putting Anthony's inheritance in jeopardy – Ronald's new wife, Phyllis, being at the marginal child-bearing age of 45. But there was no child and Anthony was given the estate in 1983, although Ronald and Phyllis remained in the chateau for a further three years.

Anthony recalls Ronald as being 'quite pig-headed' during this uneasy overlap. A new de-stemmer was denied him, for example, because the existing one had done the 1945 vintage 40 years previously and was not, according to Ronald, in need of change. 'I had to bribe the *maître de chai* to say that it had broken down,' remembers Anthony. 'The trouble is that one can't test a de-stemmer until the vintage, and so when we had a few teething problems with the new one, Ronald was absolutely delighted.'

Anthony finally took outright control on the death of Ronald in 1986, since when he has improved the quality and reputation of these previously underachieving wines dramatically. 'I take winemaking very seriously,' he says, 'but believe that wine drinking should be fun.'

Although Langoa and Léoville share the same chateau, cellars and owner (with all the winemaking taking place at Langoa), the wines are very different and are kept firmly apart. In the Bordeaux Classification of 1855 the 45-hectare (111-acre) Léoville Barton was categorized as a Second Growth while the 15-hectare (37-acre) Langoa was classified as a Third Growth. The grape varieties and the proportion in which they are grown and used are the same on both properties – 72 per cent Cabernet Sauvignon, 20 per cent Merlot and 8 per cent Cabernet Franc – although the soil types are quite different. Léoville's wines are judged to be the more elegant of the two, more complex and intense, while Langoa's are considered more approachable.

In total, 40 people are employed on the estates, with another 120 locals helping out at the harvest. 'I don't employ a full-time oenologist, though,' says Anthony, 'because in my view wine wants to be left in peace. If the chap had a wine education, he'd forever be trying to do things.'

Anthony and Eva had two children, Thomas, who went to Eton, and Lillian, who went to St George's, Ascot. ('I sent her to school in England,' says Anthony with a grin, 'when I realized that her next history lesson was entitled *La Perte du Canada*.') Thomas would have inherited the estates, but was killed in a road accident in 1990 at the tragically young age of 32. Later that year, Anthony had a striking new *chai* built at the property, which he named 'Chai Thomas'. 'I was going to list all the previous owners of the chateau,' he says, 'but then realized that Thomas's name would never be on it, so I decided to dedicate it to him instead.' Today, although Anthony is ostensibly the proprietor of Langoa and Léoville, the properties in fact belong to Lillian (now 48), with her children, Melanie (16) and Damien (14), both having been given shares. 'She's really the boss now,' says Anthony. 'I give her advice and sometimes she takes it and sometimes she doesn't.'

Despite her English schooling, Lillian – whose husband, Michel Sartorius, is French – 'is now more French than me,' reckons Anthony. Her children consider themselves French and so, after eight generations, the Bartons are finally assimilating, even though the children are being raised – more in theory than in practice – as Protestants rather than Catholics. Anthony is confident that he has passed on the estates in a healthy state, and believes that there will always be a market for fine red Bordeaux.

'I'm getting old-fashioned,' says Anthony, 'and my broad mind and narrow waist have swapped places. I realize that it is fashionable at the moment to denigrate the wines of Bordeaux and that many people are against us. The trouble is that this area produces wines of infinite variety and price, from the pretty dreadful stuff, albeit very cheap, to the pretty delicious wine, sometimes, but not always, very expensive. What happens to most of this top-quality stuff is that it goes into a cellar and never comes out again because it is too expensive to drink. However, between the cheap and not-so-cheerful and the untouchable, there are plenty of lovely wines produced in sensible quantities and sold at reasonable prices. They are not collectors' items but consumers' wines, and they deserve to be destroyed with pleasure – and replaced.'

de Ladoucette

Loire, France

E ven in the Loire Valley, where beautiful chateaux abound, Ch du Nozet's icing-sugar prettiness stands out.

Built in 1850 as a replacement for the original, smaller Renaissance model – once home to an illegitimate daughter of Louis XV – the exquisite 70-bedroom chateau and its vineyards lie just outside the town of Pouilly. The estate has been making wine for more than 600 years, and it is the largest single producer of Pouilly Fumé.

Château du Nozet was bought from the king's illegitimate daughter by Comte Lafond in 1787 and it has remained in his family for six generations. The estate is currently in the hands of the Comte's direct descendant Baron Patrick de Ladoucette. Married to Anne with two teenage daughters, Anne-Charlotte and Alexandra, 52-year-old Patrick is the epitome of old-fashioned French aristocratic chic: sophisticated, charming, witty and fluent in several languages. In fact, Patrick was born and brought up in Buenos Aires, his father having departed for Argentina in the aftermath of the Second World War. Patrick, who holds dual nationality, didn't set foot in France until he was 12. He took over the family estates at Ch du Nozet in 1972.

While his forebears produced wine at Ch du Nozet simply for their own amusement, Patrick's commercial skills and tough business sense have enabled him to be the first in his family to make a living from wine, with the estate now representing only a small part of his vinous empire.

The de Ladoucettes mainly live in Paris but, when in residence at Ch du Nozet, everything is done formally, with uniformed maids in attendance and meals served by waitresses in white gloves. The family doesn't open its home to the public, and the privilege of visiting or staying in the chateau is reserved for favoured customers, sommeliers and agents. It has proved a priceless marketing tool.

Patrick is something of a perfectionist, as is obvious from a single glance around the estate. Five gardeners are employed to tend the elegant gardens, which were laid out in 1910 by Achille Duchene, who later redesigned the gardens at Blenheim Palace. The gravel paths are immaculately raked, the yew and privet hedges tightly cropped and the lawns mown to the last millimetre (every other day,

Above: Although Baron Patrick de Ladoucette lives mainly in Paris, he is a frequent visitor to Ch du Nozet, especially at harvest time, when he takes a close proprietorial interest.
Opposite: The chateau lies at the exact midpoint of the Loire Valley, 500km (310 miles) from both the sea and the River Loire's source.
Previous page: The first glimpse of Ch du Nozet in the Loire Valley is a dramatic one.

Opposite: The aristocratic finery of the chateau itself and the elegance of family life within its walls can mask the fact that Ch du Nozet is a thriving estate and that Baron Patrick de Ladoucette is an astute businessman. There are almost 40 employees working on the wine side of the estate and 15 working in the chateau, such as carpenters, mechanics and electricians, some of whom have been with the baron for 30 years. The fleet of lorries, trucks and mowers is serviced on the estate, timber is dried and aged at the estate's own carpentry, and the state-of-the-art winery (built in 1992 at a cost of £3m) is one of the most modern in the Loire.

Below: Much to Patrick's amusement, many an unwary visitor to Ch du Nozet has congratulated him on the leafy abundance of the vines along the drive, only to discover that they are in fact blackcurrant bushes, used to make the estate's crème de cassis.

demands Patrick). He doesn't allow any flowers to disturb the formality of the design, although his wife has managed to sneak some roses in along the foot of the chateau's walls. 'Not only do they look all wrong,' Patrick exclaims, 'but when you add flowers to a garden you have to add another half dozen gardeners. I often get teased about how particular I am about things, especially in the garden, but if everything was ordinary, we'd have nothing to dream about.'

The 164 hectares (405 acres) of vineyards and blackcurrant fields – for this is Cassis country, too – are equally well maintained, with arrow-straight rows of vines and bushes separated by manicured grass paths and verges. The estate buildings are also in a pristine condition, with the cellar doors and window shutters painted in the family's old racing colours of green and white. The company's tractors and cars are similarly decorated. 'As far as I know, we're the only wine-producing company in France, apart from Ch Mouton Rothschild, to have its vehicles in company colours,' boasts Patrick with a grin.

Patrick, who is known to drive a hard bargain, has a simple business philosophy. 'I was always taught that you should never buy a tie on the day that you need one, but to stock up and buy several when you don't need one. As a result, my two adages are to buy against the market and keep well stocked.' For example, he will buy storage vats when he spots them going cheap, rather than when he needs them, as can be seen in one of the yards where two vast stainless steel vats are lying idle. Beside them is a pile of cobble stones bought from the Corporation of Lyons when the city centre was re-covered in tarmac. 'We'll use them one day,' says Patrick with a shrug. He stockpiles fuel for his tractors only when the price has fallen, and he insisted on waiting to buy his fleet of mowers second-hand only when the right opportunity arose.

The estate carpentry and workshop is another example of Patrick's business sense and attention to detail. This facility was set up on the banks of the River Loire in 1978 with wood from the family forests and elsewhere, bought against the market. Timber is aged here for up to ten years (outdoors for four years and indoors for six). The doors, windows, shutters, staircases and other accoutrements of all Patrick's estates are made and refurbished here.

'If we didn't keep these skills going, all the stuff would have to come from IKEA,' sniffs Patrick. Even the panelling for the company headquarters in Paris was made here. 'They made the door to my office of Fort Knox-like thickness because everyone says that I shout too much,' he laughs. Three

carpenters are employed full-time at the chateau alone, to ensure that the constant refurbishment of the building is just as Patrick wants it.

At Ch du Nozet, Sauvignon Blanc is the only grape grown, Pouilly Fumé being what is today termed a 'single varietal'. Half the grapes are home-grown and half are bought in from the same growers that the company has been using for the last 100 years. They make two wines: Pouilly Fumé de Ladoucette and Baron de L, a prestige cuvée that was first instituted in 1975 and made only in exceptional years.

Patrick is a firm believer in consistency; his winemaker, Joel André, has been with him for almost 30 years, and his predecessor served for a similar length of time.

'We're like an old married couple,' he laughs. 'We've had some battles, but now all is quiet. Although Joel is from Châteauneuf-du-Pape, he was charmed by the raw materials here and he's accepted the north now. Even his accent

has changed. We have nothing more or less here than other areas, but it seems to work, largely because our wine is mature, our vineyards are mature and our people are mature.'

Although Sauvignon Blanc is grown throughout the Loire Valley, Patrick believes that the fruit grown on his estate is special. 'Terroir is 60 per cent of the wine,' he says. 'Our wines are known for their subtlety, and their elegance, finesse and minerality. We've produced Sauvignon elsewhere in the Loire with the same care, but we don't get the same results.'

Patrick has used Ch du Nozet as a springboard for his wine-related ambitions elsewhere. He currently owns wine estates in Vouvray, Chinon, Sancerre, Chablis, Burgundy, Champagne and Spain (simply for producing sherry vinegar). He used to own winemaking properties in the Napa Valley and Argentina, although he is no longer active there. 'Wine is not an economic business, it's a passion, as we all know, but there must be a limit to one's passion. Besides, in a French restaurant I'd be at the back of the wine list rather than the front,' he explains. He also has a mineral water spring in France, a Cognac company and his own Cassis production, along with offices in Tokyo and Dublin.

All Patrick's wine estates have their own winemaker, something upon which he insisted in order that the identities of the regions and the wines were not compromised. 'In my view,' he says, 'it's rare to get a winemaker who is good at making both red and white wine. It's like being used to driving on the left and having to drive on the right. Whites need to be fresh and reds need to be meaty.'

Patrick's views on selling wine are as dogmatic as they are on making wine, and he is especially dismissive of supermarkets. By branching out with his other fine wines, he has been able to offer restaurants and hotels a much better deal by encouraging them to take the whole range of his wines. 'I want to stay at the top end,' he says. 'And a big range enables me to do just that. I'd have gone mad just making Pouilly Fumé in the Loire. In California or Australia you can make several different wines, something that simply isn't possible here. The only way to do it is to buy into some of the other top regions in France. And it must be the top end as I don't want my standards to drop.'

He markets his wines with considerable skill. Several of them come in old-fashioned style bottles 'so that they stand out', and his Marc de Chablis is sold only in magnums 'so that it is the most noticeable bottle on a restaurant's drinks trolley'.

Patrick likes to work alone, unfettered either by a board of directors or by family associates. Apart from himself, the only decision-makers in his organization are his wife, a finance director, a commercial director and the individual winemakers.

'I believe that unless one is on one's own, it diminishes the latitude to act,' he explains. 'If I had brothers and sisters questioning why I have five gardeners, or why I have to go to Paris all the time, there would be blood on the carpet. I couldn't have people querying everything I do. Having no board means that I am able to do what I want, when I want and where I want, although unfortunately it does also mean that there are no controls on my spending.'

Despite Baron Patrick de Ladoucette's successful incursions outside the Loire (not all of which have been well received by neighbouring winemakers who can be resentful of outsiders – even if they are French – setting up business within their ranks) he is a Loire man *au fond*.

'Ch du Nozet is where it all started for me and I see it as my home,' he says. 'We hope that our daughters will each have a place in our enterprises and that they will be happy. But although I shall continue to invest in other areas, the Loire is where I belong.'

Above: It is the proud boast that no plot among the 164 hectares (405 acres) of vines lies more than six minutes from the winery, ensuring that all the grapes are picked and pressed at optimum ripeness.

Opposite: About 100,000 cases of Pouilly Fumé are produced each year at Ch du Nozet, with a further 8,500 cases of the luxury cuvée Baron de L made in exceptional vintages. The wines are bottled on demand to preserve freshness, and the estate always keeps at least two years in stock, which puts it in a strong position should there be a poor harvest.

Pol Roger

Champagne, France

Forty-year-old Hubert de Billy is as exuberant and effervescent as the champagne his family firm produces – his

quick-fire conversation is punctuated by Gallic shrugs and snorts of bubbly laughter. As the marketing director

of Pol Roger since 1997 (succeeding his father, Christian), Hubert represents the fifth generation of his family to go

into the business of making champagne; he is the great-great-grandson of the company's founder, Pol Roger himself.

Remarkably, Pol Roger was barely 19 years old when he established his business in 1849, and it is a source of enormous pride to Hubert and his fellow descendants that more than 150 years later the company continues to flourish in his family's hands.

There is no doubting that the firm is very much a family concern: Pol Roger ran his company for 50 years until his death in 1899, whereupon the reins were taken up by his two sons, Maurice and Georges, who were permitted to change the family name to Pol-Roger by presidential decree (although the company name dispenses with the hyphen). In time, the brothers passed on the running of the firm to their children, who passed it on to *their* children, with the latest generation being represented by Hubert de Billy, Maurice's great-grandson.

As the only son among four sisters – one of whom died young – there was a certain inevitability that Hubert would join the family firm, although after his education in Reims and Paris, he did work for a short time with a Parisian real estate firm. 'That experience helped me realize that my future was with the family business,' he says now, wryly. Of Hubert's sisters, Laurence is a librarian in Paris, Veronique is a housewife and only Evelyne has joined him in the business. As befits a former employee of grand fashion house Hermès, Evelyne brings a touch of Parisian *haute-couture* glamour to her job as vineyard manager, and she cuts a stylish figure during her

regular inspections of the vines. Their cousin-twice-over, Christian Pol-Roger, is the impossibly urbane managing director, while Hubert's father, Christian de Billy, in spite of his recent retirement, continues to be involved in the company's affairs as president of its controlling board.

It may come as a surprise to learn that Pol Roger is one of the smaller champagne houses. It is also one of the very few privately owned Grandes Marques champagnes that remains, and it is a testament to the family's strength, unity, business acumen and respect for tradition that the company has remained independent for such a long time, producing wines of the highest possible quality and enjoying a formidable reputation that belies its modest size.

The firm's offices are housed in a striking 19th-century chateau, which is regarded by many as the most beautiful in the region. Its classic French exterior leaves first-time visitors quite unprepared, however, for the very English

nature of its interior. On the walls of the lobby, beneath the glassy gaze of a stuffed boar's head, the arms, badges and crests of British regiments, clubs and associations jostle for position with framed cartoons, caricatures and ancient copper-plate invoices.

The overwhelming sensation of walking into an exclusive gentlemen's club in London's West End is further compounded on entering the first room on the left, which, depending on whom you ask, is known as the English Room, the Churchill Room or the Library. Any of these names, though, would suit the charming celebration of Pol Roger's most famous devotee – Winston Churchill. This is where guests of Pol Roger are greeted, and as they sit by the sweet-smelling log fire, gazing at the English hunting prints on the walls and the Churchill memorabilia – the framed medals charting the great man's life, the photographs, the drawings and old menus – they must pinch themselves to remember that they are in northern France.

Churchill adored champagne, and Pol Roger above all other champagnes. From the time of their first meeting in 1944, he was equally smitten with Odette Pol-Roger, the striking wife of Jacques Pol-Roger, eldest grandson of the founder. Odette, who died in 2000 at the age of 89, was a great beauty whose sparkling charm and wit were the very embodiment of Pol Roger champagne, making her the ideal 'ambassador' for the company. Churchill was so in her thrall that he named his racehorse after her and promised to pay her a visit in Epernay. 'Invite me during the vintage, and I'll press the grapes with my bare feet,' he declared.

Churchill particularly liked to drink his Pol Roger by the imperial pint (a bottle size that, sadly, is no longer made but is roughly equivalent to 50cl), and it is reckoned that in the last ten years of his life, more than 500 cases of the stuff passed through his cellars. Of her father's fondness for Pol Roger, Churchill's daughter Lady Soames once said, 'I saw him many times the better for it, but never the worse.' When Churchill died in 1965, Pol Roger paid tribute to their favourite and most loyal customer by adding a black border to the labels of all their non-vintage 'White Foil' champagne sold in the UK.

Most members of the family associated with the firm live almost next door to one another in the Pol Roger equivalent of the Kennedy Compound. The complicated old property laws of Champagne required that those firms needing extensive cellars could lay claim to their title only by inhabiting houses built above them. It is not uncommon, therefore, for large families involved in the champagne trade to be immediate next-door neighbours – even today – so as to safeguard ownership of their bottle-crammed caverns below.

Famously, Pol Roger's 7km (4 miles) of cellars are colder than those of any of the other champagne houses – at 9°C (48°F) rather than 10°C (50°F). This is because they are the region's deepest, with the three different levels reaching down some 35m (115ft) below the Epernay streets. Kept in semi-darkness, the endless passages, which are piled high with maturing bottles, seem an impenetrable maze. Hubert explains that the corridors run on a grid system and are not as hard to negotiate as they seem, although even he has been known to be momentarily unsure as to his exact subterranean whereabouts.

Champagne is the most flamboyant of wines and also the acme of the winemaker's art. Only wine that comes from the strictly designated area of Champagne – some 70km (43 miles) northeast of Paris – and made solely from Pinot Noir, Pinot Meunier and Chardonnay grapes by the so-called 'champagne method' (*méthode traditionelle*) may call itself champagne. The grapes are picked and pressed, and the resulting juice then undergoes an initial fermentation. Once fermented, the wines, which may be from different vintages (unless a vintage champagne is

Opposite: Sir Winston Churchill (bottom right), the company's most illustrious customer and devotee, is warmly remembered at Pol Roger. Those who work in the vineyards are not employees of the company, but growers themselves, who, having laboured on their own vines (the fruit of which they supply to Pol Roger), bring their own tools and equipment to work on Pol Roger's.
Below: Pol Roger is the last Grande Marque champagne house to do all of its *remuage*, or riddling, by hand. There are four *remueurs* in the company, each of whom can turn between 50,000 and 60,000 bottles a day.

being produced), vineyards and grapes, are blended together. Before bottling, an additional solution of yeast, sugar and wine is added, causing a second fermentation in the bottle, which produces the bubbles. Sealed with crown caps, the bottles then mature on their sides for up to three years, after which they are gradually tilted – or 'riddled' – until vertical, causing the sediment created during the second fermentation to fall into the neck of the bottle. This sediment is removed and the bottles topped up before being corked and labelled.

It is with great pride that Pol Roger boasts of being the only Grande Marque champagne house still to do all its riddling by hand; even such traditional champagne-makers as Bollinger and Krug now use machines to riddle their non-vintage champagne, reserving the hand-riddling for their vintage wines. There are four *remueurs* working at Pol Roger, each of whom can turn between 50,000 and 60,000 bottles a day; Hubert reckons that they are so good at their job because they know that they are an endangered species.

But just because Pol Roger is traditionally minded and has resisted the lure of mechanized riddling, it doesn't mean that it hasn't embraced change in other areas, such as by introducing

Above: The gates to the chateau boast a name to conjure with.

Opposite: Since he lives only a few strides from his office, more often than not Hubert is able to have lunch at home with his wife, Delphine, a successful interior designer from Brittany, and – during the school holidays – with his three young children, Alexis, Maximilien and Victoria. Referring to the youngsters' names, their grandmother Chantal de Billy (bottom right) jokes: 'Alexis is the Romanov, Maximilien the Hapsburg and Victoria the Windsor. All we need now is a Bourbon to complete the set.' Occasionally Christian Pol-Roger (middle left), Hubert's cousin, drops in.

stainless steel for its vinification, for example, something that the company believes gives the winemaker greater control over fermentation. 'The fact is that the firm has prospered by marrying the best of the old with the best of the new,' explains Hubert. 'One of the beauties of being a family firm is that the same people are always involved and there is a great sense of continuity, something that far from deterring change, makes change all the more readily absorbed. Being a winemaker is rather a curious occupation and you need real passion and time to be a good one. Both of these commodities are most readily found within a family firm.'

Although Pol Roger produces a variety of different champagnes, including a Vintage Blanc de Blancs, a delightful, salmon-pink Vintage Rosé, a sweet and refreshing Rich and the spectacular Sir Winston Churchill Cuvée, it is the Pol Roger Brut Non-Vintage (the White Foil) that defines the company's house style. This is a blend of a least two vintages drawn from up to 30 base wines composed of roughly equal proportions of the three champagne grapes. The wine is released for sale only after it has enjoyed three years' maturation in the cellars. Hubert believes that it is a combination of several things that makes Pol Roger's wines special. 'It is the wine's roundness, smoothness and elegance that set it apart: the roundness coming from the one-third each of the three grape varieties, the smoothness coming from the longer ageing we give the wines – giving time to the time, you might say – and the elegance coming from the second cool *débourbage* – the cold settling of the grape must, which allows a slow and gentle first fermentation.'

Hubert enjoys drinking Pol Roger throughout a meal, stopping only at the cheese course. The non-vintage White Foil, he believes, goes especially well with light fish dishes and white meats, while the Brut Vintage and the Vintage Blanc de Blancs are perfect with fuller-flavoured fish dishes and *assiettes de fruits de mer*. The Vintage Rosé is an excellent accompaniment to red fruits and to puddings that are not too powerfully sweet, such as simple strawberries and cream, and the Rich is just made for *tarte tatin*. As for the Sir Winston Churchill Cuvée, Hubert reckons that this wine has the weight and body to partner grilled meats, creamy fish dishes and even roast chicken or turkey.

When he is not drinking his own product, Hubert favours fine wines such as Ch Mouton Rothschild, Ch Lafite Rothschild, Ch Cos d'Estournel, Beaune Clos des Mouches and Hermitage La Chapelle. Pol Roger has every right to be mentioned in the same breath as such illustrious names.

F E Trimbach

Alsace, France

B etween the Vosges Mountains and the River Rhine in north-eastern France, Alsace is a land of rolling hills, ruined castles and improbably pretty villages. Given the region's troubled history, which has seen it switch between French and German nationalities with dizzying regularity, it is remarkably well preserved. This bewitching place – bafflingly, all too often ignored by wine lovers – has been home to the Trimbach family for well over 350 years.

Above: Brothers Jean and Pierre Trimbach with their families on the steps of Pierre's house at the winery.
Left: Trimbach's Riesling Cuvée Frédéric-Emile is made solely from the grapes grown on the slopes overlooking the winery. It is produced from very ripe grapes, picked selectively at the end of the harvest. The fossil-flecked clay-limestone soil brings out all that is best in the Riesling, as does the ideal south and south-east exposure of the vineyards.
Previous page: F E Trimbach produces some 16 different wines a year with a total annual production of around 100,000 cases, all of which – irrespective of grape variety – is bottled in the same tall green bottles.

Documents dating from 1626 record a young man, originally from Switzerland, being recognized officially as a citizen of the small Alsace village of Riquewihr. He took as his surname the name of the Swiss village where he was born – Trimbach, which is near Basle. Jean Trimbach went on to plant vines in Riquewihr and made his living as a winemaker. He soon became immersed in local life, with both his son and his grandson not only following him into the family business, but also becoming mayors of the village.

In the 1840s the family moved to the nearby village of Hunawihr, and it was here that the founder's grandson seven times over, Frédéric-Emile Trimbach, developed the business into the present House of Trimbach. He gave the firm his initials – 'F E' – and they have been retained ever since. International acclaim for Trimbach came in 1898, when Frédéric-Emile showed his wines at the great international fair in Brussels, carrying off the most coveted prizes. From that time, on F E Trimbach has been lauded around the world as one of the great wine names of Alsace.

Soon after the First World War, the company moved to the town of Ribeauvillé, where it remains to this day. The family tradition has been proudly maintained from father to son through 12 generations of great winemakers, with Hubert Trimbach currently at the helm, ably assisted by his brother Bernard, who is semi-retired, and Bernard's sons: Pierre, the winemaker and vineyard manager, and Jean, who is in charge of sales and marketing. 'Such a successful inheritance is mostly down to luck,' shrugs the boyish Jean Trimbach with a smile. 'It just so happens that each generation has managed to keep hold of everything, while protecting the vineyards for their successors. And, luckily, everyone involved has wanted to be involved.'

Trimbach owns about 30 hectares (74 acres) of vineyards, and as its production has expanded, so it has had to buy in more grapes from outside. It now purchases about 70 per cent of its requirements, but this is not from choice: all their own land is fully planted, there are restrictions that prevent planting on new sites, and although an ailing competitor sometimes puts a vineyard up for sale, this happens only rarely. How different from the New World! The company produces about 100,000 cases a year, and whereas Alsace as a whole exports about a quarter of its total production, Trimbach exports 85 per cent, with half of its production going to the United States (where it is the best-selling Alsace producer); the rest of its exports go mainly to Scandinavia, the Benelux countries and the UK.

The company grows the full range of grape varieties that are permitted in the production of Alsace wines: Gewurztraminer, Muscat, Pinot Blanc, Pinot Gris, Riesling, Sylvaner and Pinot Noir. 'We will never grow the "Gucci" grapes,' declares Jean. 'The rest of the world can do that. We can grow so many varieties anyway, so why grow Chardonnay? Well, why die stupid? We have a wonderful niche here in Alsace and no desire to grow anything else. I taste our wines every day and every day I get excited by what I taste, as I always find something different to savour. My brother makes wines of power and elegance, and all too often, in my opinion, elegance is forgotten by winemakers. I suppose this is what they call passion – and I pray that it is passed on to the next generation.'

For many years, Alsace was the only region in France to market its wines under the name of the grape variety, rather than simply under a brand or chateau name. Customers knew exactly what they were getting, and this helped sales, especially in the United States. However, Riesling and Gewurztraminer are still too often perceived as German grapes, and it was Pinot Gris that really cracked the American market for Trimbach, accounting for 40 per cent of their sales in the United States. 'Everyone loves Pinot Gris,' declares Jean. 'Riesling can sometimes be a little too, um, intellectual.'

The company's finest wines are the Riesling Cuvée Frédéric-Emile, whose grapes are grown on the choicest slopes overlooking the winery in Ribeauvillé, and the single vineyard Riesling Clos Sainte Hune. The grapes for this stunning wine come from a 1.3-hectare (3-acre) plot in Hunawihr, which has been in the Trimbach family for more than 200 years. The production of Clos Sainte Hune, which is regarded by many as the greatest of all Alsace Rieslings and has an ageing potential of between 30 and 40 years, rarely reaches more than 600 cases a year, and often falls to as few as 250 cases. When asked what makes the wine so special, Jean shrugs and says, 'It's the grape, it's the soil and it's the microclimate. No malo-lactic fermentation and no oak-ageing. *C'est tout!*'

The company's Rieslings may appeal to the purists, but Jean believes that it is with the Gewurztraminers that Trimbach really comes into its own: the rich but dry Gewurztraminer Cuvée des Seigneurs de Ribeaupierre and the sumptuous and rare Gewurztraminers Vendanges Tardives and Séléctions de Grains Nobles.

'You need a little education to understand Cuvée Frédéric-Emile or Clos Sainte Hune. They are both connoisseurs' wines,' he explains. 'Riesling needs time, but Gewurztraminer can be drunk either young or old. To my mind, Alsace's strength lies with Gewurztraminer, because nobody in the world makes it as well as we all do here. We make great Riesling, of course, but then so do Germany and Australia.'

Legend has it that during a particularly bad vintage in the 16th century, Sainte Hune turned water from a village fountain into wine, and so it is no surprise that a grateful winemaking community built a church in her honour. This church – which overlooks the eponymous vineyard and which has wonderful views over to Germany and the three chateaux of Ribeauvillé – is used both by Catholics and Protestants on a sort of time-share basis. And it is in this churchyard that the Trimbachs, born and bred here for well over three and a half centuries, are buried.

The Trimbach family has been Protestant for 12 generations, although this is coming to an end (much to Hubert's disappointment) because both Pierre and Jean – and two of their three sisters – have married Catholics, with Pierre's and Jean's children being raised in that faith. It is not that the family is especially devout, but more that it is proud of its Protestantism in cultural terms. Indeed, Jean is fond of saying, 'Our wines are not flashy or over the top. They are pure and disciplined wines. I would say that they were Protestant wines.'

Above: The Trimbach winery is hard to miss, its prominent half-timbered gothic tower making it a familiar local landmark. Although no changes can be made to the vineyards themselves – apart from the expansion of their area by the very occasional purchase of neighbouring plots – there is always new building work and development under way at the winery.

Opposite: Alsace is a famously close-knit region, whose architecture, wines and food are arguably more readily identifiable than most in France. The Trimbachs are similarly rooted in the soil – they have been making wine in the region for over 370 years.

Opposite: Pierre Trimbach, who took over as the company's winemaker and vineyard manager in 1985.

Below: The next generation of Trimbachs. Although he is only 11, Jean's son Julien has already declared that, as the only boy in the family, he wants to be his uncle Pierre's successor as winemaker. Meanwhile, Pierre's daughter Anne (19) has announced an interest in emulating her uncle Jean by doing the company's sales and marketing.

One might imagine that a firm of such antiquity in such a well-established wine region would be stoutly traditional, but this is not so. Of course, Trimbach cannot experiment with new grape varieties, and nor does it want to, but it can be innovative in the winery. 'We're always trying to experiment with new techniques,' says Jean. 'If it's good for the wine, we go for it. Pierre and I are both very open-minded and we don't stay as still as people might imagine. We were the first in Alsace to try reverse osmosis and the first to try new *barriques*. We were the first winery here to use temperature control, and our bottling line is the finest in the region; we've had it three years and every one of our competitors has come to gawp at it.'

Jean is a dryly witty man, modest and self-effacing. But he is not without passion, especially when defending a perceived slight on his beloved wine. 'Oh, God! I've heard the phrase that Alsace wine is "the wine merchants' wine" for so long and I hate it. Why are wine merchants incapable of transferring their enthusiasm for our wines to their consumers? They've managed it with the wines of other regions. My father heard that phrase 40 years ago, for heaven's sake!'

Proud of both Alsace and Trimbach, Jean takes great enjoyment in showing visitors the winery and its ancient cellar, where many of Trimbach's past vintages lie in cobwebbed splendour, the oldest of which is 1834. 'Alsace's history has been turbulent, to say the least,' says Jean with a wry grin. 'Consequently, some of these wines are German and some of them are French. But they're all Trimbach.'

In the company tasting room beneath a sign that says 'Say no to oak, help put the fruit back into wine', Jean likes nothing more than to uncork a few treasures for appreciative visitors. He knows his wines backwards and is a gifted salesman. 'Our wines are dry, clean, pure and bright,' he explains, 'and they go well with fine food. Many wines in Alsace are too sweet, with too much residual sugar; not a good thing in my view. But not with us. We're guardians of the traditional Alsace style. We don't sell to supermarkets and therefore lose some sales, but we would rather sell to top restaurants and get our name in front of the connoisseurs.

'We like to bottle our wines early, rather than sell them early,' he continues as he opens another bottle. 'At Trimbach, we like to mature our wines in bottle for between four to five years before putting them on sale. This makes us different from our competitors, who tend to release their wines earlier. This isn't a marketing gimmick; it's just that our wines need time. Our father did the same, as did our grandfather before him. I think that our customers appreciate that we care about this.'

The future for the Trimbachs looks bright, although after 370-odd years and 12 generations, things are beginning to change. For the first time in its history the family will be Catholic, rather than Protestant, and for the first time there will be female Trimbachs working in, and owning, the company. In addition, if everything turns out as expected, the 13th generation of Trimbachs will have cousins running the company, rather than just one son or two brothers, with Jean's two children, Pauline and Julien, joining forces with Pierre's two children, Anne and Frédérique. The company is currently owned equally by Hubert and Bernard, and it will be left in equal shares to Pierre and Jean; in the French manner, their three sisters will be compensated by property or stocks.

'Who knows what will happen?' asks Jean with yet another shrug. 'We're lucky and privileged to live and work here. We're proud of our wines, but I hope not boastful. We are so lucky to be Alsaciens, and I often tell my children how lucky they are to live here. So far things have just emerged naturally in terms of family succession. I've told my children it's up to them, but that they must work hard. Very hard!'

Weingut Joh Jos Prüm

Mosel-Saar-Ruwer, Germany

H igh on the terraced hills overlooking the small riverside town of Wehlen, in the heart of the Middle Mosel, Manfred Prüm – a jolly man in his early sixties with a booming voice and an easy laugh – stands among the vines and takes in the familiar view. The endless rows of vines seem to be sliding down the precipitous slopes to meet the meandering River Mosel and, in the distance, the towns of Graach and Bernkastel can be glimpsed.

Above: 'Being a winemaker is no job for a lazy person,' says Manfred Prüm. 'I trained to be a lawyer, but I realized that wine was a full-time occupation.'

Left: The work in the vineyards is painstaking and arduous. 'The reason that our wines are of the quality they are is because we have good vineyards and we work hard,' explains Manfred. 'And clearly without the latter, there would be no point having the former.'

Previous page: From his house on the banks of the River Mosel, Manfred Prüm gets a fine view of Wehlen's bridge, beyond which stretch his family's vineyards.

On the river's southern bank, in the shadow of Wehlen's celebrated bridge, stands the Prüm family's handsome Victorian home, in which Manfred was brought up. The Mosel is slow and gentle here, and the stillness and quiet are broken only by birdsong and the splash-landings of local swans. Even the frequent river traffic is unobtrusive, with heavily laden barges and tourist cruisers slipping by with no more than a murmuring chug-chug.

'This land is dedicated to the vine,' says Manfred, making a sweeping gesture with his hand, 'and has been ever since the Romans started producing wine here 2,000 years ago. It's important to reflect upon the Roman influence and the roots of our culture. I believe that such tradition must count for something, although I am aware that it can sometimes be an excuse for immobility. My family has lived in these parts for over eight centuries – coming originally from near Aachen where there is a town called Prüm – and I can't escape the fact that my father was here before me and that my daughter will be here after me. As a result I feel that I am as much a product of this soil as my grapes.'

Manfred, who has something of a gentle, donnish air about him, is the owner-winemaker of J J Prüm, a small producer celebrated for the stunning purity and long-lived elegance of its Rieslings. Although the Prüms have been making wine here since the 18th century, the firm was founded in 1911. Johann Josef Prüm himself was born in 1873, one of seven children. Inheritance laws and conventions of the past meant that on the death of his father, the family estate was divided equally. Johann's portion was the only one to flourish and remain intact; the other six portions either failed or were broken up and sold.

This estate passed to Johann's only son, Sebastian – Manfred's father – who tended it for about 40 years. When he died in 1969, without leaving a will, his widow sat down with their four sons – Jost, Eckart, Manfred and Wolfgang – to see how best to proceed. All the brothers were agreed that there wasn't room for the four of them to work in the winery. The two eldest were already established in other professions, and it was Manfred – who had studied to be a lawyer – who was most interested in becoming involved in the business. He agreed to take on the winery provided that he was allowed to do so alone, a condition that was readily accepted by everyone else. Wolfgang joined the winery in a subordinate capacity, and although he and Manfred are now the owners of the company, Manfred owns much the larger share and remains the sole decision-maker. The estate is about 19 hectares (48 acres) in size, which is larger than it was before it was divided, thanks to shrewd purchases by both Sebastian and Manfred.

Manfred and his wife, Emai, have three daughters: Katharina (24), who studied law, Bettina (23), who is studying biology at Freiburg, and Christina (18), who has just left school and is about to start studying art and design. Katharina is expected to take over the estate in due course because, once again, it has been agreed that it is best run with a single person in charge.

'Katharina is well motivated and qualified, and I hope that she will take it on,' explains Manfred. 'She will continue her studies while growing into the estate. As regards the other two girls, we'll come to a satisfactory solution. To do a division of the estate today, as the family did in 1911, would be a catastrophe, as there is no guarantee of the families getting on. When I was younger

Opposite: The soil here is a poor-quality shale or 'rotten slate'. In the Prüm vineyards the vines are nearly always trained on poles, rather than wires, and all the picking is done by hand. The production of late-picked or botrytis-affected wines is particularly time-consuming and laborious, with each individual grape sorted by hand. The annual production is even labelled by hand (bottom right), but refreshment in the small family business is never far away (bottom left).

Below: Wine labels and capsules await the next batch of bottles.

we were forced to discuss the matter since my father didn't leave a will, but luckily we resolved it in a civil way and in a happy atmosphere, because my brothers and I all had the future of the estate in our hearts. But I don't want to leave such things to chance again, however difficult it is for my daughters to decide their futures at this young age.'

The estate encompasses some of the finest parcels in the most celebrated vineyards in the region. Only Riesling is grown here, with the average age of the vines being about 50 years. The main areas planted are in the Wehlener Sonnenuhr, Zeltinger Sonnenuhr, Graacher Himmelreich and Bernkasteler Badstube vineyards. The first two vineyards are so-named because of the vast whitewashed stone sundials placed within them in 1842 by Manfred's great-great-uncle, Jodocus, as a way of keeping his workers abreast of the time. The company manages to grow all the grapes that it needs, something that Manfred believes to be important. 'In my opinion,' he says, 'it's crucial to keep the viticulture and the vinification in the same hands.'

The vineyards are so vertiginously steep that most of the work is done by tractors with ploughs on winches, a method that is also used to transport the grapes. By necessity all the picking is done by hand, with five people working the estate full-time and up to 30 Polish workers arriving for the harvest. Some of the terraces and slopes of the vineyards look impossible to tend, so steep are they, but it is this very sheerness that gives the vines a perfect exposure to the sun, with nearly all the vines being trained on poles rather than wires.

Manfred picks his grapes late, later than most of his rivals. 'It's a risky thing to do because of the weather, but in my view there is a danger of too high a level of acidity if you pick early,' he explains. Sometimes the harvest is done all at once, sometimes there is a second picking for the sweeter wines. Occasionally, pickers even carry separate buckets for the different quality wines.

Vinification at J J Prüm is simplicity itself as Manfred believes in minimal manipulation. The grapes arrive at the winery, which is immediately adjacent to the family home, are tipped into the crusher and thence into the presses. The juice runs down to the stainless steel vats in the floor below for slow fermentation at low temperature – there are no pumps involved, just gravity. Bottling is done on a mobile bottling line, and the average annual production is approximately 10,000 to 11,000 cases. The results are classic Rieslings with great elegance, which are known for their longevity as well as for their slow development. 'If we work carefully,' explains Manfred, 'our wines have great ageing potential. I try and make this potential a reality – this thought is always at the back of my mind. Even one of our Kabinetts in a good vintage can last for between 30 and 40 years. And our Kabinetts are as important to us as our Beerenausleses. When we're at home that is almost all that we ever drink.'

Justifiably proud of his own wines, Manfred reckons that the Rieslings produced in the Rheingau, Mosel-Saar-Ruwer and the Nahe are the finest in the world and that it is impossible to imitate them. 'I have no desire to make red wine here, or to make white wine anywhere else. My place is here, making Riesling. But you must have Riesling in the right place,' he says. 'Here the grape is grown on slate and that's where the cherished minerality comes from. Long growing and slow ripening are vital, both of which you get with our moderate climate. Acidity decreases slowly and sugar increases slowly, while minerality and fruit flavours grow. Although our wines are low in alcohol, they have excellent structure and fine flavour.'

Manfred pities those winemakers who have more than one variety to tend, and relishes the opportunity to search for excellence with just his beloved Riesling. Indeed, this most engaging and enthusiastic of men only gets irritated when he hears German wines accused of a lack of variety, simply because they are made from the same grape.

Above: Freshly gathered late-picked Riesling grapes await pressing.

Opposite: There is a great sense of history, tradition and continuity in this part of Germany, where wine has been made since the Romans. Manfred Prüm enjoys the feeling that he is doing what people have done before him for 2,000 years, and is proud that his own family is documented as having lived in and around Wehlen since 1156.

'What nonsense!' he explodes. 'Of course there's variety! There will always be variety in the vineyard, in the winemaker and in the vintage, let alone in the style.' Manfred also decries those who believe that German Riesling can accompany only a limited number of foods. He enjoys claret and red burgundy when he's not drinking his own wine, but believes that Riesling can go with anything, from seafood and poultry to red meats and even cheeses. Frau Prüm is a fine cook and Manfred loves matching his wines to her dishes.

'Riesling is so versatile!' he exclaims. 'All I suggest is that one drinks a wine with sufficient age. And anyway, it's a lot harder to match red wine with fish than it is to match white wine with red meat.' For hearty dishes of venison or wild boar, for example, Manfred believes that one need look no further than a 1982 Wehlener Sonnenuhr Auslese, a pairing that works deliciously well, albeit surprisingly for those brought up to drink heavy red wines with such meats.

And, as far as Manfred is concerned, a young Kabinett is the finest of all aperitifs. 'I'm fond of champagne, of course, but it has a tendency to lift you up and – if not consumed moderately – to drop you. Riesling simply lifts you. At the moment you could do no better than a 2000 Graacher Himmelreich Kabinett. And you needn't fear driving a car afterwards since it is only 7–8 per cent alcohol.'

Manfred has an enviable existence, making a thing he loves in a place he adores. There are wild boar and deer to be hunted in the hills – the antlers and tusks in the hallway of his home testify to his prowess at the sport – and family skiing trips to be undertaken in the winter.

'I'd prefer more time for my holidays,' he laughs, 'but it's a good life living and working here. I like being in the house that I was brought up in and looking at the beautiful scenery in the way that my father did. But much as I love living here, it wouldn't be the same if I didn't enjoy my work or didn't think it important. Wine has always been important in human culture – the Greeks and the Romans even had their own gods of wine – and it is important to maintain this. The world is richer for wine and wine growers, and I felt it to be a duty – a destiny, even – to take on the vineyards. A pleasant duty, though. I've grown up here, like my vines, and this is where my heart is.'

Fattoria Le Terrazze

Le Marche, Italy

A ntonio Terni – nuclear engineer, yachtsman, winemaker and Bob Dylan fanatic – is easy to spot in the cafés in the town of Ancona on Italy's Adriatic coast. Fifty years of age, tall, slim and bearded, he will probably be wearing a yellow tartan shirt, faded blue jeans and a leopard-skin fedora, and he will definitely be drinking a quadruple espresso and be wreathed in clouds of cigar smoke.

Above: Antonio Terni and his daughter, Giulia, re-creating the cover of Bob Dylan's 1965 album *Bringing It All Back Home*.

Opposite, clockwise from top left: Prunings from the vine; Antonio's glass cake dish with the treasured hats touched by Bob Dylan himself; the wall of the winery declares its provenance; the inscrutable gargoyle that unkind wags have likened to Antonio.

Previous page: The ancient mulberry trees that line the road leading to Le Terrazze.

Antonio and his elegant English wife, Georgina, are the proprietors of the tiny Fattoria Le Terrazze, producers of bewitchingly delicious Rosso Conero DOC in the up-and-coming wine region of Le Marche. Antonio's father, Paolo, a Jewish lawyer, fled Mussolini's Italy in the 1930s and made his home in Buenos Aires, where he became a successful publisher. Antonio was born there and his family didn't return to Italy (to Milan) until he was ten. He laughs when questioned about his background. 'I'm a Jewish Italian who was born in Argentina and who is married to an English Catholic. I am like the guy in the Beatles' song 'Nowhere Man'. I don't feel any particular nationality or allegiance. Oh, except when Italy plays Argentina at football. Then I am most definitely Italian.'

The house, vineyards and farm that comprise Le Terrazze lie on the outskirts of Numana, a small fishing town on the coast some 22km (13 miles) from Ancona. Just off the road south out of town, a sweeping avenue of mulberry trees leads to the Ternis' hill-top home, behind which stand the modest winery and a barn, which once housed a silk worm factory (hence the mulberry trees). 'This barn is going to be converted into offices and a large tasting room big enough for Bob Dylan to play in,' announces Antonio with mock seriousness. The 20-hectare (49-acre) vineyard, of which only about 12 hectares (30 acres) are in production, was originally planted by Antonio's grandfather in 1882. It was nurtured by his father, who inherited it from a cousin, and taken over and completely renovated by Antonio in the 1980s. He has done some further planting recently but doesn't plan to increase production. 'I'd only have to go round the world and sell it,' he grumbles.

The Terni family home is a rambling affair. Antonio has a study on the ground floor, which leads onto a vast living room, where there hangs a 12-panelled portrait depicting Antonio as various historical figures: Rasputin, Henry VIII, Karl Marx, Jimi Hendrix, Garibaldi, Van Gogh, Verdi, Bob Dylan, Che Guevara, Merlin, Baron Münchhausen and Joshua Slocum. When asked whom she thinks her husband most resembles, Georgina ponders before replying, 'He'd like to be a bit like Rasputin, I guess, or Jimi Hendrix but, in fact, there is a bit of all of them in him.' Family portraits line the rather rickety stairs that lead up to Georgina's study, where she has her piano, and on to the bedrooms. When not ensconced here, Georgina and the couple's 18-year-old daughter Giulia live in a small flat in Ancona, so Giulia can be near her school.

Fattoria Le Terrazze produces only about 8,500 cases of wine a year, almost all of which is Rosso Conero, a red wine that has laboured for far too long in the shadow of better-known – but not necessarily better – Italian wines such as Chianti, Barolo, Barbaresco and Valpolicella. It is thanks to producers like Le Terrazze that Rosso Conero is now deservedly being given a wider currency, alerting consumers to the fact that Le Marche as a region has the potential to produce more than the wine-bar standard white wine Verdicchio.

Le Terrazze makes three Rosso Conero DOCs, named after the nearby Monte Conero, and, although a 15 per cent dollop of Sangiovese is permitted to be added, all three wines are made solely from Montepulciano grapes – the force behind Montepulciano d'Abruzzo. (Confusingly, this has nothing to do with Vino Nobile di Montepulciano, which is named after the town of that name and is made from Sangiovese grapes.) A basic but lip-smackingly full-bodied Rosso Conero is followed by Sassi Neri, named after the beach in nearby Numana that turns black in summer, thanks to the mussels that proliferate there. 'It's a rather good wine,' giggles Antonio, 'only just behind Sassicaia – well, alphabetically at least.' The third wine, Visions of J, named after the Bob Dylan song 'Visions of Johanna', is made only in especially fine vintages, the last one being 1997. All three wines go perfectly with the local specialities, such as rich pasta dishes, game, smoked meats or *porchetta* (roasted pig stuffed with onions, herbs, garlic and wild fennel). Antonio likes to serve his reds cool rather than at room temperature, which is something that inevitably sparks a good-natured debate with Georgina, who prefers the wines warmer. ('Well, warm the glass in your hand, then.' 'But I wouldn't have to if it was the right temperature in the first place.' And so on.)

As well as the three Rosso Coneros, Le Terrazze produces a single varietal Chardonnay called Le Cave and a red wine made from 50 per cent Montepulciano and 50 per cent Merlot/Syrah called Chaos, in a nod to Antonio's previous nuclear engineering career and the chaos theory. The label for this wine changes slightly every year, although it always features a geometric design based on fractal clusters. The first vintage was 1997, and it has been a great success, not least, reckons Antonio, because nobody else has created such a blend of grape varieties. Indeed, so unusual is the blend that it is unrecognized by the wine authorities, resulting in an IGT (*Indicazione Geografica Tipica*) classification, instead of the DOC (*Denominazione di Origine Controllata*) status that its quality merits.

In further homage to his hero, Antonio has released a new Montepulciano/Merlot blend named after Dylan's 1974 album *Planet Waves*. This project has the personal endorsement of the master himself, and the labels all bear Dylan's signature. Antonio can barely contain his excitement. 'Where this will lead, I don't know,' he exclaims. 'But perhaps one day Bob will buy a wine estate with me.'

There is no bottling line at Le Terrazze since Antonio hires a travelling bottler who usually takes only a few days to fill the 100,000 or so bottles that are produced each year. There are presses and a crusher, which, admits Antonio, 'are not state of the art, but they work'.

Making wine at Le Terrazze is an intimate affair, and only six people work full time at the winery, with a dozen or so others who come on board when needed. Georgina does all the accounts and sales, as well as selecting the grapes, while Antonio is in charge of marketing. The winemaking itself is in the hands of Attilio Pagli, who has been at Le Terrazze for many years, and whom Antonio has entrusted to make some serious Malbec at another project of his, Altos Las Hormigas, an estate in Mendoza, Argentina, of which he is part-owner.

Antonio neither restricts himself to Italy nor does he spend all his time thinking about wine. One of his current obsessions is olives, and he has recently planted a large number of olive trees on the estate. He already makes about 1,000 bottles of olive oil a year and would like to make more. 'I love olive groves,' he says. 'They are so much nicer to look at than vineyards, which are nothing more than green corridors.'

The Ternis have a rich life away from the estate, too. In fact, ask either of them what their passion is and, instead of wine, they would both answer 'music' – albeit music of very different styles. While Georgina listens to Mozart, Haydn, Schubert, Brahms and Shostakovitch, Antonio listens to Bob Dylan (he has well over 300 Dylan CDs), The Beatles, Pink Floyd, The Animals and Jimi Hendrix, and while Georgina relaxes by playing the piano, Antonio finds peace – even if nobody else does – by strumming his electric guitar. And where most winemakers or vineyard

Opposite: With a Bob Dylan obsessive for a father and a classical music devotee for a mother, it was inevitable that Giulia would have some musical interest. She practises here in front of Antonio's 12-panelled portrait. Below: The labels for the Chaos wines change slightly every year, although they always feature a geometric design based on fractal clusters. 'The chaos theory describes why certain patterns cannot be fully explained. And in my view no wine can be fully explained by the countless interactions between its compounds,' says Antonio. 'I've studied thermodynamics, and the fundamental principle is order here and disorder elsewhere. Hence my desk is neat and my brain isn't.'

Top: **Bundles of cuttings lie ready to be grafted onto rootstock. 'The only thing we have, with which nobody can compete, is our** *terroir*,**' says Antonio. 'Cover that with oak and so on and you lose that typicality. Markets and fashions change, and it doesn't do to follow fashion. Make a good wine and try to make it better, but make it as it should be.'**
Above: **Georgina Terni at home with Giulia. Georgina runs her own music festival, Musica Museo, which she founded in Ancona in 1997, and which specializes in promoting new, young talent.**
Opposite: **A mulberry tree shades the entrance to the former silk worm factory that now serves as Le Terrazze's winery.**

proprietors would have copies of wine magazines, such as *Decanter*, the *Wine Spectator* or *Wine*, and volumes by Hugh Johnson, Jancis Robinson or Robert Parker, Antonio's bookshelves are crammed with back numbers of *Total Guitar* and books such as *The Dictionary of Strum and Picking Patterns*, *The Art and Music of John Lennon* and *The Concise Bob Dylan*, interspersed with tomes like *Nuclear Reactor Theory* and *Exploring Chaos*.

Antonio is, to put it mildly, obsessed with Bob Dylan and is proud to call himself one of Dylan's 'Bobcats' – the term given to only the most devoted of fans. 'He is the coolest thing ever!' he exclaims, having criss-crossed the world following his hero and having seen the great man in concert well over 80 times at the last count. He wears his leopard-skin fedora in deference to Dylan's song 'Leopard-Skin Pillbox Hat' from the album *Blonde on Blonde,* and he has many such hats lying around his office, living room and dining room. A select few are displayed in a glass cake dish. 'Those are the ones that have been touched by the man himself,' murmurs Antonio reverentially. 'I always take one to a concert to throw at him, and these are ones that he threw back.'

Antonio also loves to sail and has a 6.7-m (22-ft) yacht in Numana harbour. He often takes off for a few days, sailing the 95km (60 miles) or so to the Croatian coast and back. He sometimes takes a shipmate, although he prefers to go on his own. He loves the solitude and the lack of mod cons: 'The more things you have, the more things you have to go wrong.' He likes being able to go where he wants, when he wants, being answerable to no one and having to make no decisions.

'I try not to make plans,' says Antonio, 'because if you do, the chaos theory will ensure that they will go wrong. So really I don't know what will happen to our winery. Of course, I would like Giulia to run it, or her children. If not, I have a niece I could leave it to. Or we could always sell, which would be a shame, but hardly heartbreaking.' Antonio has only recently bothered to set up a website. 'I prefer to be understated,' he says. 'And anyway, so many winery websites are boring. Too many have sites simply to be fashionable and, consequently, don't give a clear message of what they're about.'

Antonio has an appealingly laid-back, almost Zen-like, attitude to life and is no lover of ostentation. 'I was once sailing to Croatia,' he recalls, 'and kept being passed by noisy, smelly motor boats making waves. They just wanted to get somewhere and then move on, not caring whom they disrupted or annoyed. I believe that it is far more important to enjoy the journey and not to bother other people. It is surely best to be calm and to arrive quietly, without making waves and lots of excitement.

'My life is full of many pleasures,' he continues through a cloud of cigar smoke. 'Bob Dylan, sailing and wine. My father never pushed me into the wine business, and I don't believe that one should be a slave to what one's family has. I made the decision myself to take over the vineyard, and it's one of the best things I ever did. So I suppose you could say that I blame myself for my happiness.'

Kumeu River Wines

Kumeu, New Zealand

Kumeu River Wines lies on the main road running north out of Auckland, where the suburbs give way to rolling hills and green fields. Long before today's rich Aucklanders and retired dentists came here to buy their second homes, this prime farming land was settled by Croatian immigrants in search of a new life.

These exiles, most of whom arrived between the 1890s and the end of the Second World War, found work digging for kauri gum, a resin-like substance used for linoleum and varnish, which, in the early 1900s, was New Zealand's largest export. They also planted the crops they had cultivated back home: beans, garlic and vines. One such couple was Mick and Katé Brajkovich, who arrived in New Zealand from the Dalmatian coast in 1938. After a few years digging for kauri gum and working around the country in vineyards and orchards, they pooled their earnings with their son Maté and, with a deposit of £200, bought a property with a small vineyard in Kumeu. They named their fledgling estate San Marino Vineyards, and concentrated on producing imitations of sherry and port, along with a white wine made from the then ubiquitous Müller-Thurgau. It was a bucolic and picturesque spot in those days, but the meandering farm lane has since been replaced by the thundering main road and the ramshackle barn opposite the main vineyard has been usurped by a BP filling station.

Mick died in 1949, leaving his charismatic son to continue what they had started together, and to build the winery into the thriving business it is today. In 1958 Maté married Melba Sutich, whose family had also emigrated from Dalmatia. In those days, 'dallies' – as they were known – tended to stick to their own, and marriages between Croatians and New Zealanders were rare. 'I wondered why a man in his thirties and as strikingly handsome as he was wasn't already spoken for,' recalls Melba, who gave up her job as a school teacher to join him in working at the winery. 'He explained that he had wanted to get established before he got married and that when he met me he felt that the time was right. He showed me the winery and the cellars that the family had built and told me his dream was to make the best wine in New Zealand.'

Melba looked after the administration of San Marino Vineyards while Maté took care of the wine's production and its promotion. 'We put so much work into publicizing our wines at the beginning,' says Melba. 'Maté was a great character and everyone loved him. People would come from miles around to buy our wines simply because he was so entertaining and made people laugh. He had no education at all, bar going to primary school, but his marketing skills were second to none, and there's no point making a great wine – as we now are – if you can't persuade anyone to buy it.'

Despite early success, it wasn't until the mid-1980s that the winery came of age. Maté's efforts were reinvigorated when his sons joined the family firm, leading to a complete rethink of the company philosophy. They bought more vineyards and started making higher quality wines, replacing existing grape varieties such as Müller-Thurgau and Palomino with Chardonnay, Sauvignon, Pinot Noir and Merlot. In the belief that wines with Italian-sounding names didn't sell well in New Zealand, they changed the company name to Kumeu River Wines after the river, or rather stream, that runs through their garden.

Maté died in 1992, leaving Melba to become managing director, a position that she still holds. Their children, who from childhood had always helped out with odd jobs in the vineyard and the winery, as well as assisting with sales at the cellar door, make up the rest of the team. The eldest son, Michael, studied at Roseworthy in Australia and became New Zealand's first Master of Wine in 1989. He is the winemaker, while Paul is the marketing director and Milan the technical director. Marijana comes back regularly to help with tastings and events. It is all very relaxed and intimate. 'We've never had a board meeting as such,' says Melba. 'We just chat about things over lunch. There are only four of us and we trust each other's judgement so decisions are easy.'

Above: **Melba Brajkovich and her late husband, Maté, had three sons – Michael, (centre), Paul (right) and Milan (left) – and a daughter, Marijana. 'Because Maté and I never stopped working, and because I always seemed to be pregnant, the kids more or less grew up in the winery,'** she says. **'They had a lovely childhood and saw as much of their dad as they did of me. I'd park their prams beside the barrels and they'd sleep or play there while the two of us worked. They clearly absorbed a love of wine in some way because none of them could wait to come back and work here.'**
Opposite: **Melba has been managing director of Kumeu River since 1992.**
Previous page: **A cloak of anti-bird netting gives the vines of one of Kumeu's growers a ghostly look.**

When, for example, Milan, in a neat display of lateral thinking, decided to invest in around 200 sheep rather than an expensive mower, nobody questioned his decision. The sheep were turned loose in the vineyards to graze on the grass strips between the vines and by the end of the winter the land looked, says Milan, 'like a golf course'. This purchase has since become an annual event, and as a result has eliminated most of the work needed in the vineyards in winter. Not only that, since the sheep gain weight during their three-month sojourn, they are sold back at market for a tidy profit.

After further experimentation, Kumeu's 30 hectares (74 acres) are now planted with Chardonnay, Pinot Gris, Pinot Noir, Merlot and Malbec, with further lots of these grapes being bought in from six small growers. 'We grow what we like to drink,' says Milan. 'It's as simple as that. The climate is our starting point. We could grow Cabernet Sauvignon, but it's on the edge here and we've accepted that it would never be brilliant, so we don't want to do it. Quality is the key, and we'd rather sell the very best that we can make. The soil and climate suit Chardonnay down to a tee, and although everyone says that there's soon going to be a worldwide glut of the grape, we feel that there will always be a market for the top quality stuff. I can't see any other varieties being used here, and I have to say that we're more than happy with what we've got.'

Yields in the vineyard are kept low to improve the concentration of aromas and flavours, and all the grapes are picked by hand. White grapes are whole-bunch pressed – a time-consuming practice, but one that Michael believes gives the best-quality results – before being fermented in barrel. The reds are de-stemmed and crushed gently before being transferred to stainless steel fermentation tanks, followed by maturation in French oak barrels. Malo-lactic fermentation is encouraged for all Kumeu's wines, something that reduces and softens acidity while rounding out the wines' flavours.

The company produces between 15,000 and 20,000 cases per year, made up of ten different wines. Six are the Kumeu River range: a Chardonnay, a Pinot Noir, a Pinot Gris, a Merlot, a single vineyard Chardonnay called Maté's Vineyard, and a Merlot/Malbec blend called Melba. Melba wasn't at all sure

Above: In 1983 a large neighbouring vineyard was put up for sale, but it was more than the family could afford. However, the wine giant Montana stepped in to help by offering to buy any surplus grapes from them and generously handing over a cheque there and then. The purchase of this vineyard was quite fortuitous and completely unplanned. As Michael Brajkovich admits, the company would be very different now if they hadn't bought the vineyard because the Merlot that Kumeu River first made from it won them a gold medal.

Right: Maté Brajkovich, who died in 1992, was a charismatic and much-loved figure in the New Zealand wine industry. He served as chairman of the Wine Institute of New Zealand from 1982 to 1985 and was made a Fellow of the Institute in 1987.

whether to be dismayed or flattered about having a wine named after her, declaring noisily, 'I'm not dead yet!' Five more wines are sold under the firm's second label, the Kumeu River 'Village' Series: a Chardonnay, a Merlot, a Merlot/Malbec, a Pinot Noir and a rosé.

Thanks to their European background and their New Zealand upbringing, the Brajkoviches have an easy-going attitude to the winemaking differences between the Old World and the New World. 'We all feel that we are New Zealanders, not Croatians,' says Melba, 'But our heritage remains Croatian, no doubt of that, and it is a huge influence on us.' Michael and Milan have both married Croatians, and where their father, Maté, had to learn English, they have had to learn Croatian.

In essence, the family look to the Old World for their inspiration, while using New World techniques. The three brothers certainly display a very European bias in the wines they drink, favouring burgundy, especially white burgundy – with which their Chardonnays are often compared – red Bordeaux, southern French, Alsace and Italian. Maté bought a lot of European and Californian wines over the years and the boys often dig one out from the cellar, usually for a Friday lunch, when Paul and Milan will present it for Michael to taste blind, just to keep him on his toes.

'I find that a lot of New World wines don't have the "X" factor,' says Michael, 'because they have developed so quickly. We have a lot to learn from the Old World with regard to that, although I feel that often in Europe they simply try and better the previous vintage or the previous generations' vintages. Here we have no such limitations or inhibitions. We do whatever we like, how we like. I mean, in Europe they're still using cork for heaven's sake!'

And cork is something about which Michael feels strongly. In 2001, after much experimentation, he decided that all Kumeu's wines would be bottled with a Stelvin screw cap instead of a cork. He is delighted with the results. Hitherto screw caps had always been associated with cheap wines, and consumers shied away accordingly, but after several serious wineries – notably from the Clare Valley in Australia – decided to move to screw caps, others followed suit without losing customers. Michael and his brothers still bottle a handful of cases with corks for comparison, and they are in no doubt that screw caps are better, giving the wine greater vivacity and purity, without affecting its capability to age and making 'corked' wines a thing of the past. 'It has been a great success for us,' says Michael. 'Quality has become far more consistent and we haven't lost sales.'

Melba and her three sons work hard in pursuing Maté's dream of making New Zealand's finest wine – which some might argue they have already achieved – but they never let work hinder their enjoyment of life and winemaking. As Marijana says, 'Mum and the boys all get on so well and love what they're doing. They are always laughing and cracking jokes. Wine's a lifestyle thing, I guess, and it would be hard not to have fun being involved in it.'

It's not unheard of for work to be interrupted by an impromptu game of cricket played against the heavy winery doors by the brothers and their children. Even if rain threatens to stop play or, more importantly, damage the vintage, Michael refuses to get ruffled. 'There's no point in worrying about anything that you can't control, such as the weather,' he says languidly. There is many a European winemaker who worries about nothing else.

'It's a great life here,' says Paul. 'We could all have done other things. We're pretty bright and well educated and no doubt we could have become lawyers and doctors and so on. But what do lawyers and doctors do when they retire? They buy vineyards, and we're there already.'

The Symington Family
Port Companies

Oporto, Portugal

The Symingtons of Oporto are giants of the port trade. Their family company owns some of the most famous port houses of all: Dow's, Graham's, Quarles Harris, Smith Woodhouse and Warre's (trading since 1670).

They also own Quinta do Vesuvio, an estate that makes only vintage port, and have a half share in Quinta de Roriz.

There are other family-owned companies in Oporto – most notably Taylor's – but the Symington Family Port Company (SFPC) is the only one to have remained entirely in the hands of one family, having being passed down from father to son for four generations. It is also the largest port company, accounting for 16 per cent of all port made and some 30 per cent of all premium port.

The company was founded by Andrew James Symington, a Scottish wine merchant who had emigrated to Oporto in 1882, and who bequeathed the company in equal thirds to his three sons, Maurice, John and Ronald. A risky business one might think, leaving a fledgling concern evenly to three siblings but, whether by accident or design, this particular method of inheritance has worked well for the Symingtons, and each original third has continued to be represented by the three separate branches of the family. The fourth generation now runs the SFPC, in the form of six Symington second cousins – Paul and Dominic (who are brothers), Johnny, Charles, Rupert and Clare (who, although not on the board, is the first female Symington in the company), and their first cousin-once-removed, Peter, who is the last remaining representative of the third generation.

For those who dread family Christmases, weddings or funerals for fear of meeting distant relatives whom they hardly know and whose names they struggle to remember, the idea of working with their second cousins every day, living near them and socializing with them might seem a daunting prospect. But the Symingtons are living proof that families can work and play together in harmony, building up a thriving and secure business as they do so.

'It's all quite simple, really,' says Peter Symington, joint managing director and head winemaker. 'It's just that we all get on extremely well together and we're devoted to what we do.'

'It's quite a responsibility being part of a family business,' admits Dominic, the sales director. 'One can't shut the door at 5.30 and go to another life; you have to give a bit extra. But our Scottish antecedents and absorption into Portuguese-Latin culture has fostered within us all a strong sense of family. We all hang out together because we like each other, and we work together because we trust each other.'

'The informality of our business interaction also helps,' adds 40-year-old Rupert, joint managing director responsible for overall financial planning. 'We've never once had to vote on something: everything is done by consensus. Even if one of us disagrees with the others, we always go with the majority and never gloat afterwards if we're proved right.'

Johnny, joint managing director in charge of vintage port and sales, agrees. 'The family may be becoming more diverse and more loosely related by blood,' he says, 'but we all remain incredibly close. We're often mistaken by outsiders for each other's brothers, and generally it's just too complicated to explain that we're not brothers but second cousins.'

Each of the Symingtons is blessed with an easy-going charm, an engagingly self-deprecating humour and, clearly, an equable temper. On the surface they might appear to be typically British but in fact, despite having immersed themselves into Portuguese life, they have ended up becoming neither British nor Portuguese, but a blend of the two.

Below: **A cousinly lunch with (from left to right) Rupert Symington, joint managing director and financial director, Paul Symington, joint managing director and marketing director, and Dominic Symington, sales director, catching up on the day's news.**
Opposite: **Traditional stone-walled terraces in the vineyards, which made access difficult, have given way to earth-banked ones, allowing some mechanization to be used. However, much of the work and all of the harvesting continues to be done by hand.**
Previous page: **The traditional *barco rabelo* is no longer used to bring port down the Douro, although most of the port houses maintain at least one of these craft, if only for the annual race along the river.**

That the family is Catholic, on account of Andrew James Symington marrying Beatrice Atkinson, whose mother was from an old Portuguese family, meant that at least they shared a religion with their adoptive country. All the cousins working in the company were born in Portugal, as were their parents and grandparents, although all the children from the fifth generation were born in England in order to preserve their British nationality, which would otherwise have been denied them. The cousins began their education at school in Oporto, before being sent to the great Catholic public schools of England: Paul and Dominic to the Oratory, Johnny and Charles to Downside, Rupert to Ampleforth and Clare to St Mary's, Ascot. They have eschewed such schools for their own children, however, in favour of Eton, Radley and Heathfield, not least because they have all married non-Catholics, except for Charles.

Although many of the family retain homes in England, the lives of all the Symingtons are rooted firmly in Portugal, with Peter Symington's branch being the most 'Portuguese'. His children, Charles and Natasha, have married Portuguese – as he did – and their children will be educated in Oporto.

'That we are an English family abroad can be open to misinterpretation,' explains Rupert. 'It's far from being the last outpost of the Raj, but when our family started out here, Portugal was a very closed society and there was not much interaction between the British merchants and the Portuguese.' This led to a certain insularity and, ultimately, to the founding of the British Hospital, the British Church, the British School, the British Club – now amalgamated with the Oporto Cricket and Tennis Club – and the Factory House, a St James's-like club for directors of British port houses.

Above: A striking view of the Douro Valley, with some of the family's vineyards in the immediate foreground.

Right: Charles Symington hard at work. He shares the winemaking duties with his father, Peter, who is shortly to retire. 'University is all very well,' says Charles, 'but it doesn't teach you the way that learning from one's father does. He has been an amazingly successful winemaker, and I couldn't have hoped for a better start than to be taught by him.'

Far right: The garden and terrace at Dow's Quinta do Bomfim.

Where once Oporto was full of British port merchants, blenders and shippers, now only three British family-owned companies remain: the SFPC, Taylor's and Churchill Graham, and, despite Rupert's protestations, there is still a distinct whiff of colonial life. This is apparent not only in the Factory House – a vast mansion that is now home to only 22 members – but also in the Cricket Club, where, on a rainy Oporto afternoon with a pint of bitter or a pink gin in hand, surrounded by fading team photographs, sporting prints, battered silver challenge cups and the English daily papers, one could easily imagine oneself in Surrey.

Each of the Symingtons' six port houses is totally independent – with separate vineyards, winery, lodges and stocks – although they do all share the same board of directors and the same two winemakers: Peter Symington, seven-time winner of the International Wine Challenge's Fortified Winemaker of the Year (nobody else has won it more than once), and his son, Charles. The wines of each house have their own individual style and character, rooted in their history, grapes and vineyards, and the family tries hard to ensure that the wines do not compete head to head.

It would have been far easier to merge the companies and the stocks, but keeping them separate means that the company has six different port names in the market, and if times become hard again, they could always sell one of the names as a separate going concern.

In the 1950s and 1960s there was a general feeling that, as a drink, port had had its day and many of the famous houses, such as Sandeman, Delaforce and Graham, were sold off while others simply ceased making vintage port. The Symingtons, however, through diversification and innovation, not only managed to survive but also to flourish.

The Symingtons have owned Quinta do Bomfim since the 19th century and have continued to buy vineyards as they came on the market (they now own 14 between them). Instead of buying ready-made wine from outside as well, they bought unpressed grapes and made the wine themselves. They invested heavily in new machinery and state-of-the-art equipment, put in place a distribution network by buying John E Fells in the UK and set up a similar company in the United States.

In addition to making the finest of vintage ports, the company has also gone in for other, more exotic, concepts, developing trendy ports such as Dow's Midnight and Warre's Otima, both of which come in chic bottles that have won almost as many prizes for their design as the wines have themselves. They have moved into table wine production, with an everyday wine called Altano and a de luxe one called Chryseia, in a joint venture with Bruno Prats, the former owner of Ch Cos d'Estournel. They have also developed the idea of single estate 'First Growth' ports with Quinta do Vesuvio, raising a few eyebrows in the process. The SFPC has even branched away from Oporto and bought a stake in the Madeira Wine Company.

'We realized early on that we had to innovate or die,' explains Paul Symington, 'and that we had to attract new customers without scaring off the old ones. We couldn't just concentrate on the retired colonels in their clubs. After all, 47 per cent of port is drunk by women. Therefore we needed to go for fresher and sexier marketing and design. I fear that without innovation, port could go the same way as sherry or cognac, whose sales have fallen away markedly in recent years.'

Family firms are often ruined by the third generation. 'Make it; spend it; break it' is often the way, but the SFPC have turned that old saw on its head. Their secret is that all the cousins genuinely get on well and have a common sense of purpose. They have a strong work ethic and play to their strengths, with someone in the family making the wine, someone in the family marketing it and someone in the family selling it. The family tree might be becoming more diluted – and who knows how the next generation will cope or who, indeed, will be in the firm – but for the time being all in this Portuguese-English garden seems rosy.

Above: The mouth of the Pinhao river where it meets the Douro. The Pinhao Valley is one of the main areas for top-quality port.
Opposite: 'None of us were pushed into this business,' says Johnny Symington (centre), 'although it was likely that I would join, given that I was my father's only son. We've no written policy, just an understanding that's never been tested that the senior son comes into the firm if there's a vacancy. The policy on retirement is much stricter: once you reach 65 you're out, with no directorship or consultancies with the firm. It works well – after all, after 15 to 20 years working with one's father, one should have picked up the knowledge. We're not in each other's pockets away from work and we're under no obligation to each other. The bottom line, though, is that we do all get along very well, both at work and at play.'

Hamilton Russell Vineyards

Walker Bay, South Africa

T here's a touch of the Steve McQueens about 40-year-old Anthony Hamilton Russell as he speeds between

the vines on his motorbike, hotly pursued by his Jack Russell terrier (named Hamilton, of course). 'I've clocked

him doing 40kph downhill,' laughs Anthony, 'although uphill he's utterly hopeless and usually has to hitch a ride.'

Anthony is on his daily tour of inspection at Hamilton Russell Vineyards – producers of world-beating Pinot Noir and Chardonnay – of which he is the proprietor. It is a 170-hectare (420-acre) wine estate in South Africa that could claim to be among the most beautifully situated in the world. An hour's drive south-east of Cape Town, HRV lies in the enchanting Hemel-en-Aarde Valley, separated from the South Atlantic Ocean at Walker Bay by a sweeping range of gorse-clad hills and mountains.

The estate was bought in 1975 by Anthony's father, Tim, then managing director of the South African arm of advertising giant J Walter Thompson. Tim had always loved wine, and planted a few Cabernet Sauvignon and Pinotage vines in his Johannesburg garden just for fun. Having nowhere else available, he matured the wines he produced in his sauna and found, to his surprise, that they were more than palatable. Encouraged, he began to look in earnest for a wine farm. He drew a blank in the most obvious winegrowing region, Stellenbosch, and moved the search to cooler areas further south, eventually finding a farm near the fishing village of Hermanus, a place he knew well from family holidays as a child. The estate was derelict with no roads and no electricity but, undaunted, Tim planted the first vines in 1976 and released his first wines in 1981.

HRV had spectacular early successes, enabling Tim to retire to the farm in 1989, selling out of JWT the following year. Things did not go as planned however, with neither the winemaker nor the general manager of the estate appreciating the now closer proprietorial presence – indeed, both resigned. This left Tim with an unexpected management challenge. Expansion at HRV stopped, new investment in barrels and plantings was cut and wine sales slowed. Furthermore, Tim no longer had the luxury of an advertising executive's salary with which to support the business.

Rescue appeared in the form of Anthony, one of Tim's four children, then working in London for the management consultancy Bain and Co, who rose to the challenge of supporting himself and his family from a tiny business in difficulties. Anthony made one strict condition about his involvement: he would return to the estate only if he were able eventually to assume complete and total control.

Above: Anthony commutes the few hundred yards to work on his beloved old Honda XR500 motorcycle.
Right: Harvest time at the Hamilton Russell Vineyards. A team of experienced full-time estate workers does all the picking by hand.
Previous page: The Hamilton Russell estate lies in the Walker Bay appellation, the most southerly in Africa. As seen from the terrace of Anthony's house, Braemar, the view northwards across the Hemel-en-Aarde Valley is a striking one.

Tim admits that he didn't find it easy handing over the reins, although he had no qualms about selling the estate to just one of his children. 'I really felt and hoped that this was a dynasty in the making,' he says, 'but you can't always be fair in order to retain assets in a family, and I don't believe in primogeniture… It's a very broadminded father that allows the son to come back and take control,' adds Anthony with a wry smile. 'It's all very territorial, male chest-beating stuff, tied up with a sense of home and domain, and it's not easy to give up.'

Tim, quietly spoken and with immense charm, and his equally engaging wife, Athene, now live in Hermanus in the family's former holiday home, converted from a pair of fisherman's cottages. Anthony lives with his new wife, Olive, in a vast Italianate villa that he had built at the heart of the farm to serve as the estate's 'chateau' ('it cost the same to build as it would to buy a one-bedroom flat in south London'). Today the farm is a thriving concern, which has grown tenfold since Anthony's return. It produces honey, cheese and olive oil, as well as up to 8,000 cases of award-winning Pinot Noir and 12,000 cases of similarly lauded Chardonnay each year.

Although Anthony is proudly South African, he is an ardent Europhile. His house would not look out of place in the Tuscan hills, and his wines would pass muster in many a Burgundy tasting, so restrained and un-New World-like are they. Indeed, it was the 'French' style of the wines that first raised their profile beyond South Africa. As Jim Ainsworth wrote of the Pinot Noir, 'If I were a Burgundian winemaker, I would lie awake at night worrying about this wine.' Rather unfashionably for a New World producer, Anthony takes the resolutely European view that *terroir* is everything. 'I was banging on about *terroir* for ages – against the grain, I have to say – but it seemed the only way forward for a small winery. For me it is the essence of wine, and "somewhereness" in a wine is vital. We don't just want to make Chardonnay and Pinot Noir; we want to make wines that express the site and soil.'

When Tim decided to buy a vineyard site 30 years ago, he looked for somewhere with an appropriate climate, something about which he knew a fair amount, having read climatology at Oxford. When Anthony took over, it was back to the drawing board. The range was greatly reduced, and experiments were conducted on the impact of soil structure on wine style. 'In international terms we have a warm climate, although it is cool by South African standards,' explains Anthony. 'The wind off the sea is our natural air-conditioning. Our research showed, however, that it was the stony, clay-rich soil that was making our wines taste the way they do, more than the climate. When we realized that, we were able to vinify accordingly.'

Anthony's chief winemaker, Kevin Grant, has been with him ten years. 'We're not so much striving for the perfect wine as striving for the perfect expression of each vintage,' says Kevin. 'And although our wines differ between vintages, there's a golden thread linking them all – what I call the "Hamilton Russellness" of them. Getting the vineyard expression and the alchemy just right is vital to us. Our wines are restrained and noted for their minerality – their expression of origin. I think that we're getting there – although it will probably take us another 30 years to get it absolutely right.'

Old vines can be diseased on this estate, and Kevin and Anthony reckon that those aged between seven and 15 years are the best. As a result, there is constant replanting and currently only about 40 per cent of the estate is in production, although this figure should increase over the years. Despite this modest percentage, the estate does not buy in grapes from outside.

In 1998 Anthony bought a neighbouring farm, which he has called Southern Right Vineyards after the southern right whales that come each year to breed in Walker Bay. With each bottle sold, Anthony makes a contribution towards their conservation.

'For us, the donations justify the use of the name on our label,' says Anthony. He founded this estate primarily as a Pinotage specialist, convinced that the grape has the intrinsic qualities to produce truly world-class wine with a distinctive South African expression. Early results have far exceeded Anthony's expectations and the wine press has been universal in its praise, not only for the Pinotage, but also for the estate's Sauvignon Blanc.

Opposite: At the Hamilton Russell winery gentle handling and traditional vinification are paramount, with each vintage aiming for expression of origin and individuality. The winery has a close relationship with its French coopers; it buys a mix of Allier, Vosges and Tronçais oak, some of which is specially air-dried on the estate. Although Anthony hates to miss an opportunity to take his motorcycle for a spin, he still finds that the most efficient way to get around all corners of the estate is on horseback, and it is a rare evening when he isn't out riding with his wife, Olive, on their horses, Bianco and Vin Santo (bottom right).

Below: Chardonnay grapes, gathered from 18 individual vineyards, await pressing prior to barrel fermentation and nine months' ageing on their lees.

Southern Right was originally set up with Anthony's children and possible grandchildren in mind. However, like his father Tim, he believes that, in due course, the estate should go to just one of his children, rather than to all of them. 'Hamilton Russell Vineyards is a gem of an estate, and I daren't risk it being broken up by leaving it to all four of my daughters. It used to bother me that I don't have a son to pass it on to, but each of my daughters has half my blood in them, just as any son would. And just think of all the formidable women who have run – and are running – wineries around the world! My hope and desire is that the most interested and or the most capable daughter takes over from me when the time comes. Leaving it to all of them equally simply fragments the estate and is a recipe for disaster in my opinion.'

Anthony has a hugely developed sense of beauty, and he relishes the fact that unlike a centuries-old estate in Europe where nothing ever changes, he has the benefit of a blank canvas and the freedom to dictate not only what grapes are grown where and how, but also how the estate is to look. When he first took over from his father, Anthony implemented 50 visual improvements on the estate each year. This could range from planting a single tree or an avenue of trees to erecting a sculpture or building a bridge. Peripheral work has now restricted this figure but, nevertheless, he does continue to plant and build. 'I used to get depressed planting things, thinking I'd never see them develop, but look at these Lombardy poplars, how they've grown in seven years, and look at those olive trees there. They're wonderful! I really hope that we're starting something here,' he says. 'After all, the wine business isn't a business as much as an aesthetic pursuit.'

Each block of vines in the estate's vineyards is named after one of the women who has married into the Hamilton Russell family, which adds to the dynastic feel of the place. 'We had a gravestone company do the stones for us,' says Anthony, 'and they were very taken aback at the commission, thinking that we'd had a terrible number of deaths in the family.'

In 1995 Anthony built a beautiful and remote 'chapel' as a studio for his then-wife, the artist Arabella Caccia. Today it lies empty, but one day, he hopes, it will be used by his daughters. He is also building another 'chapel' in the vineyards below the house, which he calls the Millennium Chapel (building began in 2000, a fact commemorated by a carved stone in the foundations). Eventually, it will be surrounded by olive trees grown from cuttings from the Garden of Gethsemane. Anthony even plans a family burial plot beside the chapel. 'I'm not religious but I am spiritual,' he says, 'and I decided on this particular site for the chapel after I saw one of my workers praying here.'

Anthony is a provider not only for his own family, but also for the whole estate. At the same time that he built his own house, he built a crèche, a community centre and a school for the children of the workers on the estate, as well as others from nearby. There is a touch of the feudal lord about him, and he laughingly admits, 'I've got a huge chip on my shoulder about not having a 300-year-old history, so I realize I've got to create the illusion of having one. South Africa offers the possibility of an extraordinary and exciting life, and those living here should pursue the tremendous opportunities with vigour and a positive spirit!'

Anthony believes that he is on the right track with what he is doing in the Hemel-en-Aarde Valley. 'There aren't usually enormous variations between our vintages, in fact the difference between 2001 and 2002 is about as big as it gets. But with 2001 I really feel that we've arrived. This is the vintage that shows the world what we're about,' he says. When tackled about his hopes for the future, Anthony thinks for a while and gazes round his estate. 'I suppose what I really want is for our wines to continue to be like a favourite author, whose individual style you love but who tells you a different story each time.'

Above: Anthony and his mother, Athene, enjoy a glass of wine on the terrace.
Opposite: Anthony's father, Tim, is still a regular visitor to the estate that he founded, and is seen here (top left) chatting with Talita Englebrecht, Anthony's assistant of 12 years. Work on the property is never-ending, not only in the vineyards, but also in the olive groves and the hills behind the house, where there are more species of plants growing in the distinctive Fynbos (middle left), than there are in the whole of the UK. The estate is only moments from the sea, where the sandy beach is a favourite playground for Anthony's daughter Isabella (bottom left) and her three sisters.

Bodegas Barbadillo

Sanlúcar de Barrameda, Spain

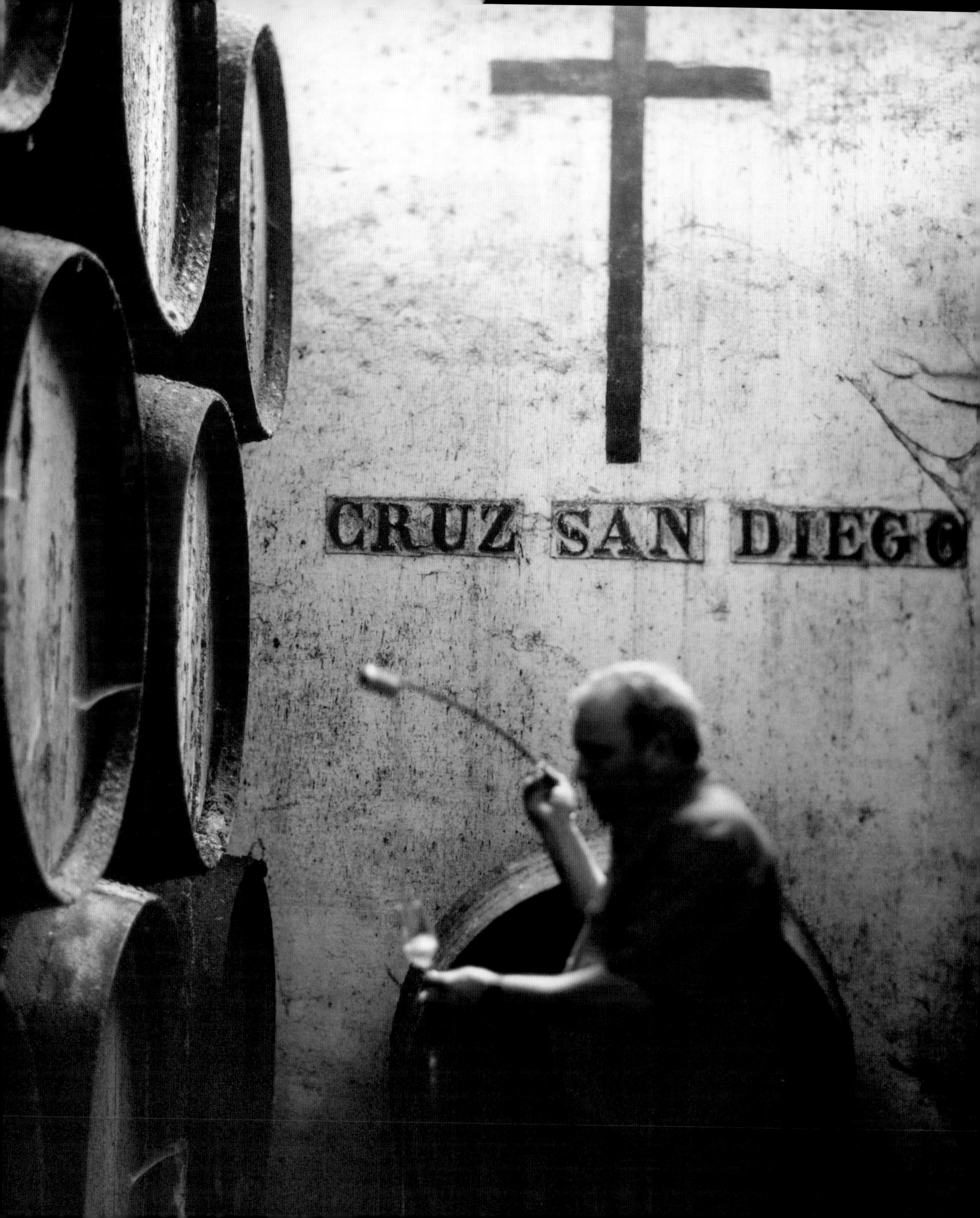
CRUZ SAN DIEGO

D espite his advancing years, and the fact that he has officially retired, the diminutive and immensely dapper 81-year-old Don Antonio 'Toto' Barbadillo still makes his way to the offices of his family firm each day. As the former president and general manager of sherry producers Bodegas Barbadillo, he likes to keep in touch with the gossip as well as taking the time to peruse the newspapers in his book-strewn, picture-crammed office.

With a wicked smile and a glint in his eye, Toto still has a way with the ladies, and when he arrives at the offices each morning he makes even the stoniest-faced employee smile with his flattery. He has clearly inherited this skill with words from his late father, Don Manuel Barbadillo Rodriguez, who was one of Spain's most celebrated poets. Known in the company simply as 'the Poet', Don Manuel was Toto's predecessor as president of Bodegas Barbadillo.

The company was founded in 1821 by Don Benigno Barbadillo and his cousin Don Manuel López Barbadillo, who were both working in Mexico for an uncle until Mexico's war of independence with Spain caused them to return home. They chose to settle in Sanlúcar de Barrameda, where the Guadalquivir River meets the sea, in what 'the Poet' called the 'Corner of the Sun', and here they founded the sherry-making company that bears their name.

Although Bodegas Barbadillo produces the whole range of sherries – from the light and dry Fino, through the darker and medium-bodied Amontillado to the sweetest Cream and the richest Oloroso – the company is best known for its Manzanilla. Since launching the first bottle of its Divina Pastora Manzanilla in 1827, Bodegas Barbadillo has grown to become the largest – and, arguably, the finest – producer of such wine. This lightest, driest and most austere of sherries is produced only in Sanlúcar de Barrameda, where the unique microclimate and, it is said, winds from the sea, cause a layer of yeast – known as flor – to grow, imparting a delicate salty tang to the wine.

In Spain, Manzanilla is the classic accompaniment to tapas. The word 'tapa', which means literally 'lid' or 'cover', originated from the practice of placing small slices of Serrano ham over the glasses, or copitas, of sherry to prevent dust from falling in them.

'Dust on the ham is fine, but not in the sherry!' exclaims Rosario Barbadillo, Toto's niece and the company's PR manager. 'Manzanilla is so versatile. It cleanses the palate between tapas and enables one to switch between fish and meat without difficulty. It also has another wonderful quality,' she adds, laughing. 'One can drink any amount of Manzanilla without really getting drunk or troubling the breathalyzer. Or getting a hangover. It's all to do with the effect of the esters and the flor on one's system and the flor's plentiful supply of vitamin B6, which is the ideal agent for breaking down the alcohol in the liver. You can even put it on cuts and abrasions to make them heal. It is, after all, only a version of penicillin.' It is a dangerously persuasive argument.

Bodegas Barbadillo's three main brands of Manzanilla are Solear and, produced for the domestic market only, Muy Fina and Eva. Solear was created in 1943–4, after most of the company's wines had been looted by

troops during the war. One of the few untouched bodegas was one that produced Manzanilla Pasada, a very fine sherry, and it was decided to use this as the base for Solear. The brand has recently been relaunched in a chic and elegant bottle and, interestingly, the company has gone back to stopper corks after having used screw caps for many years. Even though the company believes that screw caps guarantee quality and reliability, as well as making the sherry taste fresher and more vibrant, most wine drinkers still associate screw caps with cheap wines.

Bodegas Barbadillo owns some 500 hectares (1,235 acres) of vineyards, which are spread out over two estates – Gibalbin and Santa Lucia – in an area known as Upper Jerez. The company's wine cellars are scattered throughout the town of Sanlúcar, and cover an area of well over 75,000 square metres (807,000 square feet), with a capacity of 35 million litres (7¾ million gallons), which makes them by far the largest cellars in the region.

The company's offices are based in the Palace de Cilla, built in 1773, an ornate building that once belonged to the archbishops of Sanlúcar. A stone staircase off a beautiful flagstoned courtyard leads to embossed wooden doors, and it is behind these that the offices – crammed with family photographs – are situated. 'The Poet', who joined the firm when he was 18, died here in his study at the age of 96, and the room has been left exactly as it was on that day – except for his desk, which has been removed to the recently established Museo de la Manzanilla. This museum and the company's new shop stand in the shadow of Sanlúcar's ruined castle, in the grounds of which there stands a bust of 'the Poet', who is greatly revered here as a national hero.

As well as a bottling line and a laboratory, there are several separate bodegas in the complex of buildings that surrounds the museum. One of these is Moorish in style – the only such one in Andalucía – and it is here that the barrels of Manzanilla mature. In another bodega situated only yards away – this one neoclassical in style – lie the barrels of Fino where, remarkably, no flor will grow because of the influence on the air and microclimate of the ruined castle that looms over the road.

Left: Part of the so-called 'Sherry Triangle', which comprises the growing districts of Jerez de la Frontera, Puerto de Santa María and Sanlúcar de Barrameda. The region is blessed with an ideal porous and lime-rich soil known as *albariza* and 3,000 hours of sunshine per year – perfect growing conditions for the Palomino grape. Below: The vast Cathedral Bodega, where the fermented and fortified wines mature in American oak barrels. Thanks to Sanlúcar's unique microclimate, it is here that the essential flor grows on the surface of the wines, imparting its distinctive flavour.

Nothing exemplifies better how delicately balanced the conditions must be for flor to grow and for Manzanilla to be created. The most recently constructed bodega, where the young wines are first brought from the winery, was built in 1980. Here they are fortified and moved to the various other bodegas, depending on whether they are to become Finos, Manzanillas or Olorosos.

The barrel-filled bodegas are wonderfully atmospheric, but none more so than the so-called Cathedral Bodega, or Cathedral of Manzanilla. This spectacular building was constructed in 1876 and its towering columns make it the highest bodega in the region. Circular holes pierce the tops of the pillars in order to allow the air to circulate more freely, encouraging flor, and there are shutters and iron grilles on the windows to allow in the air, but not the sun.

After the death in 1837 of Don Benigno, the co-founder of Bodegas Barbadillo, the company passed first to his children and thence to his grandchildren and great-grandchildren. Today the company remains in the family's ownership, with 100 family shareholders and a board of directors consisting of nine men and two women, all of whom are members of the family either through birth or marriage. In typically Spanish fashion, though, there are three men on the board who are not shareholders themselves but who represent the women who are. This board, or *consejo*, meets once a month, although it has no say in the day-to-day running of the company. 'I must stress that it is a very well-managed company,' says Toto, 'and having a family board and outside

BODEGA DEL TORO

Barbadillo

general managers – of whom we have had only two since I retired – works extremely well for us. However, I haven't failed to notice that what I managed to do here for 40 years as president and general manager now seems to need some 22 people!'

With Toto's retirement, there are no longer any members of the family in executive positions within the company, and being a Barbadillo no longer guarantees a job within the firm. Rosario Barbadillo has the highest profile post as the PR manager, with special responsibility for the new museum and the shop, while Antonio Barbadillo Jnr is one of the sales managers, and María Eugenia Barbadillo Vidaurreta is the general manager's secretary.

'Now the family is so big and so diverse I no longer know everyone, and I must admit that the company feels much less family-like than it once did,' says Toto. 'But the family ethos is vital and I am proud that Bodegas Barbadillo is, and will continue to be, 100 per cent family-owned. The general managers who make the big decisions are no longer from the family, it is true, and that is a shame, but, although I have devoted my life to this company, I have no children and so that's how it has to be.'

Times have been hard for sherry producers, with falling sales, and different companies have weathered the storms in different ways. In the 1970s, Toto dreamed up the idea of making a still, dry white wine entirely from the main sherry grape, Palomino. Fellow sherry producers thought that he was crazy and laughed in his face. But nobody is laughing now, except Bodegas Barbadillo – all the way to the bank – since Castillo de San Diego has become the best-selling white wine in Spain, with over six million bottles consumed every year. Toto would be the first to admit that it is an everyday wine, but it is clean, fresh and well made, an ideal aperitif or accompaniment to Spanish tapas.

Toto is confident that his company has the wherewithal to survive sherry's current dip in popularity, a decline that he believes will only be temporary. 'There has been a big push to sell sherry in greater volume,' he says, 'something that has led to a fall in quality, in my view. In the past, when we sold in bulk, we never knew who our end consumer was, but once we started to bottle our own sherries and sell direct, we came to know and understand our customers. But then the supermarkets stepped in and obscured them again, with their insistence on 'Buyers' Own Brands'. With their fierce marketing, competition became terrible. Sherry used to be an expensive wine, but no longer. Now the wines can't reach the price they should for the work that goes into making them. Bodegas Barbadillo will recover, but our weakest competitors won't. This will give sherry a new image – properly priced fine wines existing side by side with the 'Buyers' Own Brands'. Even so, without Castillo de San Diego, we certainly wouldn't have survived.'

Following the spectacular success of this enterprise, Bodegas Barbadillo has branched out in new directions: a joint venture in Ribera del Duero with the Vegas family making a red wine from 100 per cent Tempranillo, called Vega Real, and, more laterally, producing the highest quality Serrano ham. Vega Real is rather New World in style – rich, jammy and juicy – and aims to be the red counterpart to Castillo de San Diego.

The UK, Germany, Holland, Belgium and the United States remain sherry's biggest export markets. The success of Castillo de San Diego has given Bodegas Barbadillo cause for great optimism, as have their initial forays into the so-far untapped markets such as Russia and Eastern Europe. Toto Barbadillo looks to the future with confidence.

'Castillo de San Diego's creation might look like a brainwave now,' he says, 'but we did it originally because we had too much wine on our hands. Vega Real will, I hope, be similarly successful for us, and I suppose you could say that these are my legacies to the company.'

Opposite, clockwise from top left: The Bodega del Toro is the oldest of the company's 17 cellars and is where the cousins Don Benigno Barbadillo and Don Manuel López Barbadillo produced their first sherries; the Sanlúcar church next to the winery; a bas-relief of Don Manuel Barbadillo Rodriguez, 'the Poet', who, as well as running the company for many years, was a prolific author, writing some 90 books of poems, novels and biography; although the 500-litre (110-gallon) barrels are sourced from abroad, full-time cooperage is needed to cope with their repair and renovation. Below: The three members of the Barbadillo family who still work for the company: María Eugenia Barbadillo Vidaurreta, Rosario Barbadillo and Antonio Barbadillo.

Bodegas del Marqués de Vargas

Rioja, Spain

The title of Marqués de Vargas was created more than 300 years ago, so it is perhaps understandable

that the current incumbent, Pelayo de la Mata, is momentarily unsure as to exactly which number

marqués he is. 'Mmm, I could have sworn that I was the 11th,' he laughs, as he seeks clarification in a leather-

bound reference book on Spanish nobility, 'but I see here that I am, in fact, the 13th. It is so confusing!'

Since Spanish titles pass through the female line and this title has gone through five different families since its creation, it's no wonder that Pelayo has lost count. The volume confirms that he is also the 7th Conde de San Cristobal.

Pelayo certainly looks the part in his grey flannel trousers, cashmere shooting jacket, Turnbull and Asser shirt and silk tie. He is fluent in both English and French, he is a yachtsman of note, a celebrated shot – who numbers King Juan Carlos among his regular shooting companions – a keen golfer and a member of the exclusive Nuovo Club in Madrid. As one might expect, Pelayo's manners are immaculate, and he can be excused the occasional elegantly stifled yawn, for at the age of 57 he and his wife of 25 years, Ana María, are proud first-time parents of 15-month-old twin girls, Ana Teresa and Mencía.

Pelayo is chairman of the family company, Varma – the name is formed from the first syllables of 'Vargas' and 'Mata' – which imports wines, spirits and foods into Spain and boasts an impressive annual turnover of £130m. The

Above: Pelayo de la Mata, the 13th Marqués de Vargas, with his wife, Ana María, and their twin daughters, Ana Teresa and Mencía. Opposite: Pelayo and his family spend most of their time in Madrid, but visit La Hacienda de Pradolagar during the summer and for occasional weekends. The hacienda has just been completely refurbished and is often used for entertaining wine merchants, sommeliers and agents visiting the estate. Previous page: The view from La Hacienda de Pradolagar, northwards across the vineyards towards the mountains of Navarra.

company was founded by his late father, Hilario, to serve as the distribution arm for Bodegas Franco Españolas, of which he was then chairman and majority shareholder.

After graduating with a degree in economics from Madrid University and then spending a year in New York on a traineeship in wine research with Seagram, Pelayo joined the family firm as its marketing director. He took to the role with relish. 'Since our key brands were the likes of Drambuie, Mumm champagne, Cutty Sark Scots whisky, Remy Martin, Seagram's VO and Wyborowa vodka, I resolved to visit as many restaurants, bars and nightclubs as possible,' explains Pelayo with a grin. 'It was important to see how our brands fared and to meet the people who served them and drank them. I must admit, though, that I also wanted to make a name for myself in the trade and to be a figure in my own right rather than just "the son of…".'

For six years, until the death of his father in 1976 led him to take over as chairman, the dashing young aristocrat selflessly haunted the watering holes of Madrid and beyond, often in the company of his youngest brother. 'It was a tough job,' he jokes, 'but somebody had to do it!'

Above: 'My life is full,' says Pelayo. 'I read, play golf, sail, shoot, act, listen to music. I also now have my daughters. Such things keep you young. Too many people I know retire then die. I was always told that one isn't human until one has written a book, planted a tree and become a parent. I've written many articles (although not a book, I admit), I've planted many trees and I've now become a parent. My girls are like me – open and happy.'

Left: The hacienda is where Pelayo and his siblings grew up and it still feels like home, with family portraits lining the walls.

Pelayo's most personal project since becoming chairman of Varma has been the development of his family's vineyards at La Hacienda de Pradolagar, which lies in the heart of the Ebro Valley, just outside Logroño. The area is known locally as 'Los Tres Marquéses' because the properties of three winegrowing noblemen lie next to one another: Marqués de Murrieta, Marqués de Vargas and Marqués del Romeral. Pelayo's great grandfather – Felipe de la Mata, the 10th Marqués de Vargas – first planted vines on the estate in 1840, although in those days the grapes were sold to other producers as the family made no wine of their own.

Pelayo's father often dreamed of making wine here, though, and even went so far as to register the Marqués de Vargas title as a brand name and trademark in the 1970s. 'It isn't often that you have a brand name existing almost 20 years before the product came into existence,' laughs Pelayo. But it wasn't until the 1990s, long after Hilario's death, that this dream became a reality, with the creation of Bodegas y Viñedos del Marqués de Vargas.

'While my father was chairman of Bodegas Franco Españolas he felt that to make his own wine with his own name on the label would be unfair competition,' explains Pelayo. 'We started to make wine firstly because it was my father's idea and secondly because I wanted to keep his name alive. Because he was so loved and respected I knew that I couldn't do something mediocre, but I believe that if you follow your heart and your passion, you will have great success. This isn't Bordeaux, it is Rioja, but in a short time we have had a wonderful reaction to our wines, although that is not to say that we can't do better. We've only been going eight years after all. But I think that what we're doing here is worthy of my father.'

The estate has dramatic views to the north across the plains towards the snow-capped mountains of Navarra, but its position is somewhat spoiled by its proximity to the main Bilbao to Zaragosa highway, which thunders past only metres away. The hacienda is where Pelayo and his six brothers and sisters grew up, and he admits to a strong sentimental attachment to the place. Recently refurbished under the guidance of Pelayo's youngest sister, Isabelle, the house now serves partly as

a summerhouse and weekend retreat for the family, and partly as a venue for entertaining business associates and customers. It is beautifully accoutred with family portraits, comfortable sofas, antique furniture and large fireplaces. There are nine en-suite bedrooms (all with monogrammed towels and toiletries), a living room, a conservatory, a vestibule, a hall, a dining room and a book-lined library with many framed scrolls and charters beside photographs of Pelayo in his yacht and chatting at a shoot with the King.

Immediately adjacent to the house stands the winery, which was built in 1989. Antlers – belonging to stags shot by Pelayo – line the entrance hall, along with portraits of Pelayo and his grandfather and great-grandfather. A picture of Hilario is soon to be added, so that the four people whom Pelayo regards as having founded the estate will all be represented: 'All the links in our chain,' as he puts it.

There are 16 stainless steel fermentation tanks, one for each parcel in the vineyard, which are picked and vinified separately. There is a vast area for ageing barrels. 'It's too big, we slightly miscalculated,' confesses Pelayo. 'But if we ever buy any other vineyards, it'll be able to cope as it has a 500,000 bottle capacity.' There is a high-tech tasting room and in the packing area bottles are stowed in smart wooden boxes – 'just like they do in Bordeaux' – emblazoned with the M and V design topped by a marqués's coronet.

The first vintage was produced in 1991, with the wines launched in 1995. The 65-hectare (160-acre) estate grows Tempranillo, considered Spain's best red wine grape, Mazuelo, Graciano, Garnacha and others – 'By "others" we mean Cabernet Sauvignon,' whispers Pelayo – and produces three wines: Marqués de Vargas Reserva, Marqués de Vargas Reserva Privada and Hacienda de Pradolagar Reserva Especial, made only in fine years.

Above: Pelayo is keen to develop wine tourism on the back of his wines' success. There is a new airport no more than 2km (1½ miles) away from the hacienda, which at present serves only Barcelona and Madrid but has the potential for foreign flights. 'The food here is great, the wines are great, the golf is great, the shooting is great, the Guggenheim and shopping in Bilbão are great, and the restaurants and bars in Logroño are great. What could promote our wines better than a weekend spent here?'

Opposite: 'It was a spiritual thing to develop the winery,' says Pelayo. 'I wanted to do something in memory of my father. One shouldn't do things just for money but because one believes in something, and I believe in tradition and continuity and honouring one's family and forebears. In any case, if you strive to be the best in the world at something – as we are here – you will always make money.'

'The brand name is all important,' says Pelayo. 'Of course I want people to like Marqués de Vargas but not necessarily to think of it as a Rioja – although I don't want to hurt Rioja's feelings. Vega Sicilia, a wine of astonishing personality, is our model. It is a great wine, much admired, but nobody thinks of it as a Ribero del Duero.'

Bodegas y Viñedos del Marqués de Vargas is owned mainly by Pelayo, his three sisters and one of his brothers, but in order to finance the building of the winery and its cellars, shares were also sold to their old friends, the Giro family and to José Bezares, the managing director. It is a small company, employing only 11 people, with extra help drafted in at vintage time. As José Bezares explains with a laugh, 'I'm the managing director, the financial director, the commercial director, the assistant to the winemaker and the drinks server.'

The company also makes a white Rias Baixas from Galicia in northwest Spain – a 100 per cent Albariño called Pazo San Mauro – and a red Ribera del Duero called Conde de San Cristobal (after Pelayo's second title), the first vintage of which was 2003. Pelayo hopes to add a fourth winery to the portfolio; for a while he was flirting with the idea of setting one up in Chile, but these plans are currently on hold. He also has hopes for developing wine tourism in Rioja, something that he believes has great potential. Other than that, he remains content.

'I love life. I try hard at everything that I do, be it sport, hobbies or work. I simply will not accept unhappiness. If I ever fail, I just move on. I think that recognizing one's good fortune is the key to happiness and we shouldn't take things for granted. One should be ambitious, yes, but one should be grateful and not let ambition get out of hand. Ana María and I desperately wanted our own family as I'm one of seven and she is one of nine. Now that we've succeeded, my remaining hope is that I live long enough to see my daughters marry. As for everything else, I shall do the best I can – the rest is in the hands of God.'

Chateau Montelena Winery

Napa Valley, USA

Jim Barrett appears every inch the Californian; with his weather-beaten face, rolling gait, denim shirt and leather waistcoat, he looks as if he has just walked off the set of a Western. In fact, Jim was born in Chicago and worked as a highly successful attorney in Los Angeles, until his head was turned by thoughts of owning a winery.

In the late 1960s, while suffering what he terms 'a bad case of industrial burn-out', Jim came to the Napa Valley for a restorative weekend with a friend, and promptly fell under the valley's spell, as many people do. 'I thought, hey, I'd like some of that,' he recalls. 'It was certainly a helluva lot better than the Los Angeles ant hill I was chained to.' It then took Jim three years' hunting before, in 1972, he came across the neo-Gothic pile that is Chateau Montelena. 'It may have been ghost-ridden and spider-infested, and somewhat run-down and overgrown, but I fell in love with it and its location, and bought it on the spot.'

Chateau Montelena had originally been founded in 1882 by Senator Alfred L Tubbs, a San Franciscan entrepreneur. Believing that the Napa Valley was the finest place in California to plant grapes, Tubbs bought a 101-hectare (250-acre) estate just north of the small town of Calistoga, famed for its mud baths and gushing geysers. His model for all things was France, and he planned to make his wines as French in style as possible. To that end he imported French vines, a French winemaker and even a French architect to build him a 'chateau' in a manner suitable for an important wine estate. By 1896 Chateau Montelena – named by Tubbs after Mount St Helena at whose foot the estate lies – was the seventh largest winery in the Napa Valley, producing some 60,000 cases a year.

The estate flourished for barely a quarter of a century, though, until the imposition of Prohibition in 1920 led to its closure as a winery. After the repeal of Prohibition in 1933, some half-hearted attempts were made to re-open the winery, but any grapes that were harvested were sold to other wineries or to home winemakers. In 1958 the Tubbs family sold the estate to a Chinese-American couple – Yort and Jeanie Frank – who, having no interest in wine, saw the property simply as a beguiling and peaceful spot in which to retire. The Franks' lasting legacy to the property grew out of Yort's attempt to build a moat around the chateau, in the belief that every castle should have one. The rocky soil thwarted his efforts, and he created instead what came to be known as Jade Lake, a Chinese-inspired water feature complete with a miniature island.

It looked as if Chateau Montelena's winemaking days were over forever, until slim Jim Barrett rode into town and bought the estate in 1972. From the very beginning, Jim had a simple philosophy. 'Make the best possible wines. Period.' The elderly vines were grubbed up, the vineyards were cleared and replanted, and the winery was filled with state-of-the-art equipment. Jim also gathered a fine winemaking team around him, headed by Mike Grgich, who had learned his trade with Robert Mondavi.

Above: **Judy and Jim Barrett with Daisy.**
Right: **A block of Cabernet Sauvignon vines. Clover and mustard are planted throughout the vineyards to add nitrogen to the soil. Each block of vines is picked and vinified separately so as to keep their individual characteristics separate until blending.**
Previous page: **The Napa Valley can get cold during the night, especially in clear weather when cool air – trapped by the warmer air above – is prone to settle on the vines. In order to stop damage to the buds or the fruit, scores of smudge pots such as these are lit among the vines, while wind machines with vast propellers are fired up to keep the air circulating.**

This page: Carved into the north side of a rocky hill, the chateau forms its own man-made cave, and what appears to be the front door leads instead to the cellars. **Right:** Bo Barrett with his wife, Heidi, and their younger daughter, Chelsea.

At the start of Jim's tenure, while he was waiting for the new vines to bear fruit, all the wines on the estate were made from grapes bought in from other growers in the valley. One of these wines was a Chardonnay, the 1973 vintage of which is still spoken of in awe, thanks to a remarkable tasting held in Paris in 1976. Steven Spurrier, then a young Paris-based wine merchant and educator, organized a tasting where four top white burgundies and four of the finest crus classés clarets were pitched against six Californian Chardonnays and six Californian Cabernet Sauvignons of similar standing. The tasting panel comprised nine of the most distinguished French wine experts of the day. What happened next was to have far-reaching consequences, not only for Chateau Montelena, but also for wineries elsewhere in California and, indeed, throughout the New World. When the ballots were cast – the wines having been tasted blind – it was discovered that Chateau Montelena had come out top. The judges had all given the wine their highest marks, convinced that they were tasting the finest of white burgundies. As Jim Barrett says, 'Not bad for kids from the sticks.'

The importance of this event can hardly be overstated because, although Californian wines and those from elsewhere in the New World were known to be improving in quality, for the first time Europeans were forced to take notice of what their competitors were doing. So thrilled were the Americans by this event that *Time* magazine famously ran an article on the tasting, entitled 'Judgment of Paris', which brought the story a wider audience.

Head winemaker Mike Grgich stayed at the winery until 1976, and was succeeded for the next four years by Jerry Luper. Hovering in the wings was Jim Barrett's son, Bo. Now Bo is the first to admit that he used to be something of a ski-bum. 'I got involved in wine to avoid getting a proper job,' he laughs. 'I told my father that I was going to be a surfer or a skier, which didn't seem to bother him at all, although he insisted that I got a job to support that sort of lifestyle. So, I did some construction work and helped out here at harvest time.' Soon, however, he found himself more and more drawn into the workings of Chateau Montelena and before long he was assistant to Jerry Luper. Indeed, so confident did Bo become that in 1980 he went to his father and asked to be made head winemaker, concerned that Jerry wasn't taking the winery in what he believed was the right direction. Jim laughed at the suggestion, not only because of his respect for Jerry's work, but also because he was disquieted by what he saw as Bo's insubordination. In any event, Jim had no wish to give the job to Bo simply because Bo was his son; if he was the right man for the job, and if there was a vacancy, that would be another matter.

Bo quit the winery in disgust and travelled round Europe in a battered VW camper van, turning his hand to a bit of freelance winemaking as he toured through Rioja, Tuscany and southern France. On his return to America he made straight for Idaho, intent on making his living as a ski guide in the

winter and a fishing guide in the summer. It took him six months to realize that he would never earn enough money to survive. So, in 1981 he returned to California, his arrival coinciding with harvest time and, at Jerry's invitation, he spent ten days helping to gather it in. Not long afterwards Jerry was unexpectedly offered an unmissable opportunity elsewhere and, in a display of magnanimity, he suggested to Jim that Bo be his replacement. Jim finally agreed, and Bo has been the hugely successful – and greatly admired – winemaker at Chateau Montelena ever since.

True to Alfred Tubbs's founding wishes, Chateau Montelena remains about as European as a Californian winery can be, and Jim regards the estate as 'a First Growth in the Bordeaux tradition'. It produces five wines each year: Montelena Estate Cabernet Sauvignon, Napa Valley Cabernet Sauvignon, Napa Valley Chardonnay, Montelena Estate Zinfandel and Potter Valley Riesling. Only Cabernet Sauvignon, Cabernet Franc, Merlot and Zinfandel are grown on the estate's 49 hectares (120 acres), with both Riesling and Chardonnay being bought in from long-standing and trusted growers. In a good year, the total annual production reaches about 35,000 cases.

Each of Chateau Montelena's vineyards produces completely different tasting grapes, as the *terroir* differs quite dramatically throughout the estate, with three main soil types in evidence: alluvial, sedimentary and volcanic. The grapes within each of the vineyards – and indeed blocks within the vineyards – are picked and vinified separately in order to maximize their differences and keep their individual characteristics separate until blending. Almost all the vineyard work is done by hand and no chemical pesticides are used – the estate prefers to employ three-quarters of a million ladybirds, brought in each year by the crate-load, to do the job instead. Similarly, no chemical fertilizers are used, and chicken manure, being the chosen agent, is traded for cases of wine (although the exact rate of exchange remains somewhat vague).

That *terroir* is everything is often perceived as a very European view, but it is at the heart of the estate's philosophy. As Bo Barrett puts it, 'We've always allowed the vineyard to follow its natural progression. We're stewards of the grape and our job is to usher it into the bottle. It's the soil that makes Chateau Montelena, Chateau Montelena, and our philosophy is "keep it simple, stupid" and just concentrate on what we're good at.' And so it is that the estate has never been tempted to grow any grapes other than the ones they do – apart from a brief flirtation with Sangiovese. 'The right grape in the right place is the key. We'd rather grow what we're good at and leave others to grow what we're not so good at,' says Bo.

Most unusually for a Californian winery, Chateau Montelena sells a proportion of its wine *en primeur*, via its so-called 'futures' programme. This is very much a Bordelais practice and one that Bo Barrett heartily endorses. 'We take what is good from European wine regions and not what is bad. It's the same with our winemaking, and our customers love it. We're in this business for the long term and we want our customers to believe in us and trust us. We want them to be able to buy our wine in the easiest and most advantageous ways – and why shouldn't they do well out of us? My father and I want people to drink our wine, not just keep it in their cellars. Why not drink it? Why, you might get hit by a bus, and I'd hate to die not having drunk our '78 Cabernet or '87 Chardonnay!'

Chateau Montelena fairly burst onto the scene in 1976 and the quality of its wines has never wavered since. Jim Barrett built around him a strong team, and in his son he has a world-class winemaker. Given that Bo is married to Heidi Petersen-Barrett – the much-lauded winemaker at top boutique winery Screaming Eagle – there is a good chance that their daughters, Remy and Chelsea, have inherited their gifts. In addition, Bo has a son, Seamus, from an earlier relationship, who is a recording engineer but might yet turn his hand to winemaking.

Chateau Montelena is the happiest of wineries, where every worker regards himself or herself as part of the 'Chateau Montelena family', and where continuity is the key. 'I'd no idea this was going to be a great winery,' says Jim. 'I just fell in love with the beauty of the place. I was a lawyer in LA for 28 years and spent my life putting frowns on people's faces. Now I'm putting smiles on them.'

Opposite: Chateau Montelena is a microcosm of California's ethnicity: a French chateau with a Chinese lake owned by an Irish immigrant family. 'My father came over from Ireland in the womb,' says Jim, proudly. Indeed, the Barretts' St Patrick's Day parties are legendary: Jim's wife, Judy, cooks corned beef and cabbage, Jim bakes the soda bread, and the winery's celebrated Chardonnay, coloured with green food dye, flows like water. Below: Jim and Judy Barrett, who are often seen walking around the estate, live only a few hundred yards from the winery in a striking modern house on the so-called Bee Hill.

Directory

Berry Bros. & Rudd
3 St James's Street
London SW1A 1EG, England
Tel: +44 (0)870 900 4300
Fax: +44 (0)20 7396 9611
orders@bbr.com
www.bbr.com
Please visit the website for information and opening hours of the BB&R shops in London, Basingstoke, Heathrow, Dublin and Hong Kong.

Bodegas Barbadillo, p 134
Luis de Eguilaz no 11
Codigo postal 11540 Sanlucár de Barrameda
Cadiz, Spain
Tel: +34 (0)956 38 55 00
Fax: +34 (0)956 38 55 01
barbadillo@barbadillo.com
www.barbadillo.com
Visits on Monday to Saturday at 12 and 1. For information and reservations contact reservas@barbadillo.com.

Bodegas del Marqués de Vargas, p 142
Grupo Vinicola Marqués de Vargas, S.L.
Carretera de Zaragoza, Km. 6
26006 Logroño – Zaragoza, Spain
Tel: +34 941 26 14 01
Fax: +34 941 23 86 96
bvargas@jet.es
Visits by appointment only.

Brown Brothers, p 10
Brown Brothers Milawa Vineyard Pty Ltd
Milawa
Victoria 3678, Australia
Tel: +61 3 57 20 55 00
Fax: +61 3 57 20 55 11
info@brownbrotherswines.co.uk
www.brownbrothers.com.au
The winery is open to the public for tasting and also has a restaurant, the Epicurean Centre.

Brown Brothers Wines (Europe) Ltd
River View Lodge
Ray Mead Road
Maidenhead
Berkshire SL6 8NJ, England
Tel: +44 (0)1628 776 446
Fax: +44 (0)1628 776 136
info@brownbrotherswines.co.uk
www.brownbrothers.com.au

Château Climens, p 42
33720 Barsac
Bordeaux, France
Tel: +33 (0)5 56 27 15 33
Fax: +33 (0)5 56 27 21 04
contact@château-climens.fr
www.château-climens.fr

Châteaux Langoa and Léoville Barton, p 62
33250 St Julien Beychevelle
Bordeaux, France
Tel: +335 56 59 06 05
Fax: +335 56 59 14 29
chateau@leoville-barton.com
www.leoville-barton.com
Visits by appointment only.

Chateau Montelena Winery, p 150
1429 Tubbs Lane
Calistoga
CA 94515, USA
Tel: +1 (707) 942 5105
www.montelena.com
The tasting room is open daily, 9.30–4. Tours are by appointment only.

de Ladoucette, p 70
Château du Nozet
Pouilly-sur-Loire 58150, France
Tel: +33 (0)3 86 39 18 33
The winery is open for tasting and tours all through the year. Please phone for details.

de Ladoucette Paris
42 Avenue Victor Hugo
75116 Paris, France
Tel: +33 (0)1 45 00 31 31
The shop is open Monday to Saturday 10.30–2 and 3–7.

Domaine Daniel-Etienne Defaix, p 50
Domaine du Vieux Château
23 Rue de Champlain – BP 50
89800 Chablis, France
Tel: +33 (0)3 86 42 42 05
Fax: +33 (0)3 86 42 48 56
chateau@chablisdefaix.com
www.chablisdefaix.com

Domaine Faiveley, p 56
Bourgognes Faiveley – BP 9
21071 Nuits St Georges Cedex, France
Tel: +33 03 80 61 04 55
Fax: +33 03 80 62 33 37
bourgognes@bourgognes-faiveley.com
www.bourgognes-faiveley.com

Fattoria Le Terrazze, p 102
Via Musone 4
60026 Numana (AN), Italy
Tel: +39 071 7390352
Fax: +39 071 7391285
a.terni@fastnet.it
www.fattorialeterrazze.com
The winery is open to the public every day except Sunday during the summer and Saturday for the rest of the year.

F E Trimbach, p 86
15 Route de Bergheim
68150 Ribeauvillé, France
Tel: +33 03 89 73 60 30
Fax: +33 03 89 73 89 04
contact@maison-trimbach.fr
www.maison-trimbach.fr
Tastings on Monday to Friday, 8–12 and
1.30–5.30.

Hamilton Russell Vineyards, p 126
Hemel-en-Aarde Valley
PO Box 158
Hermanus 7200
Western Cape, South Africa
Tel: +27 28 312 3595
Fax: +27 28 312 1797
hrv@hermanus.co.za
Open Monday to Friday 9–5; Saturdays 9–1.

Kumeu River Wines, p 110
550 State Highway 16
PO Box 24
Kumeu, New Zealand
Tel: +64 (0)9 412 8415
Fax: +64 (0)9 412 7627
enquiries@kumeuriver.co.nz
www.kumeuriver.co.nz
Open for wine sales Monday to Friday 9–5.30;
Saturdays 11–5.

Leeuwin Estate, p 18
PO Box 724
Fremantle, Western Australia 6160
Tel: +61 8 9430 4099
Fax: +61 8 9430 5687
info@leeuwinestate.com.au
www.leeuwinestate.com.au
The winery is open to the public daily 10–4.30
for tours and tastings. The Leeuwin Restaurant
is open daily for lunch and Saturday evening for
dinner. Alfresco concerts are staged in summer.

M Chapoutier, p 34
18 Avenue du Docteur Paul Durand – BP 38
26600 Tain L'Hermitage, France
Tel: +334 75 08 92 61
Fax: +334 75 08 96 36
chapoutier@chapoutier.com
www.chapoutier.com
Tastings at the cellar door Monday to Friday
9–12.30 and 2–7; weekends 10–1 and 2–6.
Tours and private tastings by appointment
Monday to Saturday.

Pol Roger, p 78
Champagne Pol Roger
1 rue Henry Lelarge – BP 199
51206 Epernay Cedex, France
Tel: +33 03 26 59 58 00
Fax: +33 03 26 55 25 70
polroger@polroger.fr
www.polroger.com
Visits by appointment only.

The Symington Family Port
Companies, p 118
Travessa Barão de Forrester
Apartado 26
4401/997 Villa Nova de Gaia, Portugal
Tel: +35 1 22 377 6300
Fax: +35 1 22 377 6301
www.symington.com
www.thevintageportsite.com

Graham's Lodge
Quinta do Agro
Rua Rei Ramiro
4400-281 Vila Nova de Gaia, Portugal
Tel: +35 1 22 377 6356
In summer, open seven days a week, 9.30–6;
in winter, open Mondays to Fridays, 9.30–1
and 2–5.30.

Viña Errázuriz, p 26
Avenida Nueva Tajamar 481-Torre Sur Suite 503
Las Condes
Santiago, Chile
Tel: +56 2 203 6688
Fax: +56 2 203 6689
wine.report@errazuriz.cl
www.errazuriz.com
Visits by appointment only. Contact Mercedes
Espindola: mespindola@errazuriz.cl

Weingut Joh Jos Prüm, p 94
Uferallee 19
54470 Bernkastel-Wehlen, Germany
Tel: +49 65 31 30 91
Fax: +49 65 31 60 71

Acknowledgments

This book would never have happened without the enthusiastic support of the families featured. I was shown great kindness during my travels and I am immensely grateful for the time and effort that they put in, making my – already delightful – job so much easier. To them all, an enormous thank you.

I am also hugely grateful to Simon Berry of Berry Bros. & Rudd, and Lorraine Dickey of Conran Octopus, again, without whom…

Karis Hunt of Storm Communications was invaluable in getting me started on the New World leg of my journey, and Judith Murray of Greene & Heaton was, as usual, unstinting in her encouragement.

I would very much like to thank the Conran Octopus team: Chi Lam, Helen Ridge, Sam Chick, Angela Couchman and the remarkably patient and lovely Zia Mattocks for all that they have done to make this book look so beautiful. Similarly, I can't thank the inimitable Jason Lowe enough for his spectacular photographs.

Finally, I would like to thank my wife, Marina, for her unceasing support, and to congratulate my second son, Ludo, for tactfully managing to remain *in utero* until I got home from my world tour.